Praise for *Law* …

'This book is a powerful testament to the truth that Australia – the lands, seas, waters and rivers, islands and skies – are imbued with First Nations' laws. It proves that our laws are not lost or distant but are being practised everywhere, in ceremony, performance, dialogue, and legal and political decision-making, weaving ways of being into existence, maintaining our cultures, country and life as they have done for millennia. Our laws are forever present and provide the pathways for all Australians to truly learn how to belong to this continent.'

—June Oscar

'This is an important book! While deeply researched, it has been presented in a way that makes it easily accessible to the general reader, and it is perfectly attuned to the present moment of truth telling which has arisen in the wake of the Uluṟu Statement of 2017. No other current work has been able to so comprehensively explain the significance of traditional law in all its manifestations and provide us the means to understand The Way of the Ancestors.'

—Henry Reynolds

Praise for the First Knowledges series …

'This beautiful, important series is a gift and a tool. Use it well.'

—Tara June Winch

'An in-depth understanding of Indigenous expertise and achievement.'

—Quentin Bryce

'Australians are yearning for a different approach to land management. Let this series begin the discussion. Let us allow the discussion to develop and deepen.'

—Bruce Pascoe

'These books and this series are part of the process of informing that conversation through the rediscovery and telling of historic truths with contemporary application … In many ways, each individual book will be an act of intellectual reconciliation.'

—Lynette Russell

'These First Knowledges books are proving among the most fascinating and important titles I have ever read; an astounding gift of wisdom delivered with generosity and optimism, offering no less than a new vision of what Australia is, and what it can be … they deserve to change minds, lives, and hopefully the development of Australia itself.'

—Jez Ford

LAW

Readers are advised that this book contains the names and images of people who have passed away.

LAW

The Way of the Ancestors

MARCIA LANGTON
& AARON CORN

Thames
&Hudson

national
museum
australia

First published in Australia in 2023
by Thames & Hudson Australia
Wurundjeri Country, 132A Gwynne Street,
Cremorne, Victoria 3121

thamesandhudson.com.au

26 25 5 4

Thames & Hudson Australia and the authors wish to acknowledge that Aboriginal and Torres Strait Islander people are the first storytellers of this nation and the traditional custodians of the land on which we live and work. We acknowledge their continuing culture and pay respect to Elders past, present and future.

ISBN 978-1-76076-282-7 (paperback)
ISBN 978-1-76076-283-4 (ebook)

A catalogue record for this book is available from the National Library of Australia

This project has been assisted by the Australian Government through the Australia Council, its arts funding and advisory body.

Front cover: *Lady Karma* by Danielle Gorogo

Series editor: Margo Ngawa Neale
Cover design: Nada Backovic
Typesetting: Megan Ellis
Editing: Katie Purvis

Printed and bound in Australia by McPherson's Printing Group

FSC® is dedicated to the promotion of responsible forest management worldwide. This book is made of material from FSC®-certified forests and other controlled sources.

For the Old People.

To our family and friends everywhere, especially Ruby and Melinda, who gave us the knowledge and permission to write this. And to all those who taught us, and whose contributions to this book we acknowledge and appreciate.

NOTE ON STYLE AND SPELLING

We follow standard English rules for capitalisation. We do not privilege words borrowed from English with initial capitals, as our book is predicated on encouraging understanding far more important and illuminating legal terms in Australia's Indigenous languages. All Indigenous names and other words are rendered in their established orthographies at the time of writing, not their Anglicised legacy spellings, as we fully support Indigenous groups working to encourage literacy and consistency in their own languages and dialects. Common archaic and variant spellings are noted throughout the book.

CONTENTS

FIRST KNOWLEDGES

MARGO NGAWA NEALE, SERIES EDITOR

This book is a powerful testament to the enduring laws that have governed life in this country for millennia. It is also a testament to the limitations of the imposed laws that have attempted to usurp all that existed before and govern this country in contravention of the laws of the land and her people. However, as so convincingly proposed in the book, these two systems now must find ways of working together for all Australians. With the goodwill, intelligence and leadership currently being exhibited by our Indigenous leaders with the call for a Voice to Parliament, and the active hearing they are getting, there is indeed new hope.

Law: The Way of the Ancestors is a timely call to action with its well-argued recognition of Indigenous law as being fundamental to Australian nationhood, offering us the gift of exchange and a social contract for a unified future. It traces the laws of the ancestors, reveals many profound differences between Indigenous and Western laws, and makes plain the absolute necessity of the inclusion of Indigenous law in the modern laws of this country.

One truth revealed here is the law's deep connectivity to every conceivable aspect of life across time, space and place, as a consequence of being a system of law that was created by the ancestors, or creator beings, and not by mere mortals. It was created by something bigger than humans – forces that Aboriginal societies refer to as ancestral forces – and is a system that has enabled Aboriginal and Torres Strait Islander people to have the longest continuous human occupancy of any place on Earth. As Pintupi elder Timmy Payungu Tjapangarti said to anthropologist Fred Myers, 'The Law was not our idea.'[1] The notion that Western law comes primarily from humans and not ancestors, and that it is written in something as disembodied and dislocated as books and then deposited in buildings that sit atop land that has nothing to do with the stories of law within that land, is unfathomable in the Aboriginal worldview. Aboriginal law is written in the land. It is as ancient as it is permanent.

A vital difference pointed out by authors Marcia Langton and Aaron Corn is that the Aboriginal definition of 'law' equally includes culture. Law and culture are inseparable – one is the other. And country holds all knowledge as an integrated whole, not compartmentalised into separate disciplines.

Another profound revelation that may surprise many readers is the notion that traditional knowledges and law systems, as spoken about in this book, are as alive and well today as they were yesterday. They permeate all aspects of people's lives, whether people recognise it or not. As the authors so succinctly put it, 'The way of the ancestors is not in the past. It is not remote or distant.' The ancestors' laws are present and active daily. Law is fundamental to everything we see and experience and is all around us – whether in a public mural, a Welcome to Country, a smoking ceremony, announcements by media presenters and airline attendants acknowledging country, an Aboriginal design on a brochure or T-shirt, or a performance by

Bangarra Dance Theatre. All are governed by law and have to be sanctioned by the right people, for the right reasons, according to law.

As Marcia and Aaron also point out, law is practised in ceremonies in many different forms today, which are often propelled by 'leaders resourcefully drawing on their knowledge of ceremonial law in response to changing circumstances and new challenges.' This is evident in festivals such as Garma in north-east Arnhem Land and Milpirri at Lajamanu in the Tanami Desert, in the music of Yothu Yindi, in the teachings of Steven Wantarri 'Wanta' Jampijinpa Pawu from Lajamanu, and in the art of Brisbane-based Jennifer Herd. Constant negotiations between Aboriginal and Torres Strait Islander people and modern governments on native title, treaty, constitutional recognition and water rights, and negotiations with mining companies, are further evidence of the presence and principle of Aboriginal law. Who has the right to speak about all its complexities and variations is always at the forefront.

Being from an oral culture, Aboriginal knowledge is an embodied and integrated system that has proven to be the most enduring human knowledge system that we know of. Aboriginal visual work is categorised in the Western world as 'art', but it is beyond art in the Indigenous world. In a non-textual oral culture, our 'art' functioned then as it functions now – as visual documents that serve as articles of law, constitutional charters and title deeds to land, among other things. It is well known that many, if not most, Aboriginal art works speak for the land and the sea. This truism was recently echoed by contemporary artist and law man Djambawa Marawili, who said, 'Land and sea can't talk; we have to talk for them.'[2]

Just as Aboriginal people have always used the visual and performative to practise and transmit law consistent with an oral culture, in this book Marcia and Aaron frequently draw on visual and performative expressions to explain law to readers. They brilliantly decode the major law painting *Possum and Wallaby Dreaming* by the late Warlpiri artist and law man Michael Jakamara Nelson (c. 1946–2020),[3] which is the basis for the epic 196-square-metre mosaic in the forecourt of Parliament House in Canberra. As Marcia and Aaron point out, Nelson's work offers important insights into 'how good governance and decision-making can be understood from a Warlpiri perspective ... in ways that both pre-date and continue to parallel the democratic processes in Parliament House.' They add that it is one of the many Indigenous governance structures that 'are still largely unrecognised by the Commonwealth of Australia.' The painting and mosaic are complex, but their intention is to teach.

Through Nelson's painting and mosaic, the authors graphically demonstrate how the kinship system works at one level through the cooperation of discrete groups in ceremonial practice. It shows the inseparable affinity between people and their ancestral animal beings – possum and wallaby in this case – whose tracks are depicted coming from the four corners of the canvas to meet at this place of ceremony in Canberra, and simultaneously depicts a Warlpiri *Jardiwarnpa* ceremony. It also refers to the political representatives that come from all corners of Australia to Parliament House to meet and do the important business necessary to govern. This is also what happens at First Nations ceremonies. Marcia and Aaron unravel the complexity of this imagery, as far as it can be unravelled, and weave it through many chapters of the book, thus grounding the concepts of ancestral law in the tangible ceremony Nelson's work articulates.

Though most readers may be aware of Aboriginal documents of protest as a series of separate moments, this book highlights the connections between them. The pivotal moments connected include the Yirrkala Bark Petitions (1963), the Barunga Statement (1988), the Elcho Island and Yirrkala Petitions (1998) and others that have led to our current watershed moment, the Uluṟu Statement from the Heart of 2017, which is actively being addressed by the Labor government under Anthony Albanese.

As with other books in this series, we have opted for co-authorship to offer a broader range of perspectives and knowledge from different cultural backgrounds, lived experiences and research. We acknowledge the expertise of knowledge holders from both Aboriginal and Western disciplines and the power that comes from such collaborations, which resonate in the context of this book on law and its call for the amalgamation of voices in the Australian Constitution. Marcia and Aaron, as long-term collaborators, have drawn on their extensive Indigenous engagements over decades to provide a lens through which we can view law practice from the desert to the sea and from remote to urban communities. Arnhem Land, the Central Desert and the Kimberley in particular are focused upon, as are the distinctive regional legal systems in eastern and western Cape York Peninsula, in north-west Queensland, Victoria, the Torres Strait Islands and much of New South Wales.

This is the sixth book in the First Knowledges series of big reads in small-format readers. *Law: The Way of the Ancestors* takes us deep into the heart of country, to the body of the ancestors, and thus effectively becomes the metadata for the other books in the series. It was to be the last, but there is now such a hunger for Aboriginal and Torres Strait Islander knowledges that the series has been extended to ten volumes. Maybe the series, like the songlines, will never end. Each title is timely and, as such, has in varying degrees become a call to action. This book is the very foundation of all other subjects discussed in the series. Using the body as an analogy, as limited as it may be, law provides a skeletal structure that holds us and our society upright, determines the shape of our world, and is immutable. The flesh, on the other hand, is more malleable and can change according to circumstances and pressure. It moves and varies in shape, texture and tone from body to body and from place to place, but always within the limitations imposed by the skeleton.

Ancestors are responsible for Sky Country – the subtitle of *Astronomy*, the fourth book in the First Knowledges series, which deals with Indigenous astronomy. It calls for the restoration of the skies and warns us of the risk to our stories that reside in the celestial domain as collateral of the country below. *Plants: Past, Present and Future*, the fifth in the series, offers us a portal to country and different ways of connecting to it. *Country: Future Fire, Future Farming*, the third in the series, demands that we look anew at our continent and its vegetation through Australian eyes and not continue the destructive practices of the colonisers. *Country* was written in the aftermath of the 2019–20 bushfires, just as this book on law was written in the midst of the promise from the Albanese government to create a Voice to Parliament. The second book in the series, *Design: Building on Country*, shows the importance of buildings and other human-made structures being extensions of country, and the need for us to design spaces as collaborators with country and not as usurpers. The first book, *Songlines: The Power and Promise*, is similar to this book on law in that it, too, establishes the foundational truth about how all knowledge resides in country, as do the ancestors. *Songlines* also gives insights into how a culture can retain and pass on knowledge from generation to generation over millennia without the written word, and how the practices of Indigenous peoples in Australia compare with those of other Indigenous peoples.

Law: The Way of the Ancestors, like other books in the series, shows how traditional knowledge, beliefs, systems and practices inform contemporary life for Aboriginal and Torres Strait Islander peoples – and, indeed, for all people who have the will and knowledge to take them on, to listen and to learn. In fact, this kind of respectful engagement could be the path to true belonging in Australia; the A<u>n</u>angu elders with whom I worked on the *Songlines* exhibition at the National Museum of Australia in 2017 certainly felt so. They were content to share the continent with newcomers, but stressed that they had to learn Indigenous stories beyond the last 250 years or they would never take root, would only ever be a transplant. This resonates with Marcia Langton's commitment to everyone knowing their history. She initiated Ngarrnga, the Aboriginal and Torres Strait Islander Curricula Project, at the University of Melbourne because of her firm conviction that 'Every Australian student is entitled to know the truth about their country.'[4] This series hopes to contribute to that aspiration.

As strongly urged in this book, the values and insights offered by the ancestors and the law of this land hold benefits for everyone and have the capacity to make the world a fairer, more just and more equitable place for all. Furthermore, the authors write, 'these systems of law were developed over many millennia and are tied inextricably to the original ancestors who shaped Australia and birthed its Indigenous people.' *Law: The Way of the Ancestors* is 'a gift to Australia. Instead of looking to its colonial past, Australia's origin story can be found here, in its own deep history.' The authors rightly claim that such a legacy deserves to be preserved and lived, to enable us to face the challenges of our age.

1

PERSONAL PERSPECTIVES

MARCIA LANGTON

Not until my adulthood did I realise that the special rules of Aboriginal life in Indigenous communities were laws. I was admonished as a child for walking in front of elders. I was not allowed to sit on their beds or swags, and I was not allowed to speak while adults were speaking.

These may seem minor rules, but they were only a few of the many that I remember from the time when my family lived in south-west Queensland, on the edge of town in a place officially designated as a native camp. The hours from breakfast to dinner I spent with other children, although there were jobs to do. The adult world was a great mystery to me. I was fascinated by the concerns and rituals that involved the adults when they were treating sickness or worrying about spirits, sweeping the dust in the camp area, or sitting for long periods in silence.

By day, in school, I was forced to listen to a fantasy about Australian history, and Indigenous people in particular, that made me suspect that what was written in books about Australia were elaborate lies. What I learnt about being Indigenous was plainly a lie, because none of the people I grew up with resembled in any way the supposed 'savages' who rampaged through the pages of my schoolbooks. White Australian law and history said that we had no conception of law, no ideas of property, and certainly no property laws.

In my adulthood, I came to realise that this was not the truth. I came to understand that the denial of the existence of Indigenous laws was a grand injustice that was as harmful as the violence and brutality against Indigenous people that Australian history books so systematically denied.

In 1981, I attended a conference in Townsville, Queensland, where I met the Torres Strait Islander intellectual, teacher and litigant Eddie Koiki Mabo. A conference called 'Land Rights and the Future of Australian Race Relations' was held at the Douglas campus of James Cook University from 28–30 August 1981; participants discussed strategies for bringing about a definitive High Court decision on land rights. Mabo, then living in Townsville, spoke at the conference and also met with people who were keen to form a legal team to litigate his ideas about native title.[1] He was the first person I had met who clearly articulated the fact that Indigenous laws exist. The paper he presented at the conference, 'Land Rights in the Torres Strait', was subsequently published as a book chapter,[2] and ten years later, his ideas laid the basis for the famous case that bears his name, *Mabo v Queensland (No 2)*, in the High Court of Australia.[3] The concept of native title envisioned in this case succeeded in the High Court and was recognised as a form of native title arising from traditions and customs.

That Indigenous customary rights to land had pre-existed and, under certain conditions, survived British sovereignty was recognised in Australian common law. Native title, which could now be recognised and protected under common law, was recognised by the High Court as having 'its origins in … the traditional laws acknowledged and the traditional customs observed by the indigenous inhabitants of a territory' within Australia.[4] Still regarded as almost revolutionary in legal circles, the High Court decision changed the relationships between Indigenous people and other Australians irrevocably. Moreover, the ruling overturned the concept of *terra nullius*, which was the prevailing legal doctrine that Australia had been nobody's land upon British settlement in 1788.[5]

Terra nullius was a fiction of imperial laws developed during the British Empire's expansion across the globe. The term means 'land belonging to no one'. It presumed that the Indigenous peoples found by the British on other continents were so devoid of government and laws that they were deemed too 'inferior' to establish a treaty with the Crown. This was not the case in the North American colonies, for example, where, although British laws and government were installed in the lands of Indigenous peoples, their sovereignty and rights to the land were partially recognised, and, later, treaties were settled.

One of the many proponents of this racist attitude to colonised societies was the British legal expert, judge and politician William Blackstone, who argued that there were 'ceded' (surrendered) and 'conquered' (taken by force) colonies.[6] Australia was deemed to be a ceded colony until the High Court overruled this legal nonsense in *Mabo v Queensland (No 2)* in 1992. Of the fiction of terra nullius, it was stated in the *Mabo* case that:

> The facts as we know them today do not fit the 'absence of law' or 'barbarian' theory underpinning the colonial reception of the common law of England. That being so, there is no warrant for applying in these times rules of the English common law which were the product of that theory. It would be a curious doctrine to propound today that, when the benefit of the common law was first extended to Her Majesty's indigenous subjects in the Antipodes, its first fruits were to strip them of their right to occupy their ancestral lands[7] ... Whatever the justification advanced in earlier days for refusing to recognise the rights and interests in land of the indigenous inhabitants of settled colonies, an unjust and discriminatory doctrine of that kind can no longer be accepted.[8]

Many years after the Townsville conference, when I was a junior anthropologist, I was living in Alice Springs. My university training included reading the works of anthropologist WEH Stanner, who had described a Yolŋu *makarraṯa* dispute-settling ceremony he witnessed in north-east Arnhem Land in the Northern Territory.[9] Among Stanner's writings is also an extraordinary biographic account of Durmugam, a Ngan'gimerri man whom he befriended in 1932 on the Daly River in the Northern Territory (Figure 1) at the end of a fierce battle between two groups, conducted by pairs of men armed with spears rushing at each other in a crowd of more than 100 combatants. There were no mortalities, but many painful flesh wounds. Amid the noise and dust, Stanner's attention was drawn to Durmugam, an 'Aboriginal of striking physique and superb carriage who always seemed pinned by an unremitting attack. He seemed, as far as any individual could, to dominate the battlefield.'[10] Stanner recounts that when 'the battle died', this tall warrior smiled and 'asked me in a most civil way if I had liked the fight'.[11]

As with several other groups from the Daly River region, the Ngan'gimerri people had been displaced from their land and their rituals were no longer performed. As a man, Durmugam was initiated into the 'secret rites of the older men' of the Victoria River region, where he travelled with other Ngan'gimerri and Wagaman youths on a grand adventure. There, he came 'for the first time into intimate association with an Aboriginal High Culture',[12] Stanner wrote, as distinguished from everyday kinship and marriage rules.

Stanner had stumbled into the chaotic world of opium, alcohol, venereal diseases and social upheaval that 'contemporary life had become for the surviving Aborigines', yet he wanted to discover the 'unspotted savage'.[13] He reported that Durmugam and his fellow initiates were 'fired' by Indigenous law, 'and also felt under some kind

FIGURE 1: A portrait of Durmugam, a Ngan'gimerri man that WEH Stanner met, befriended and photographed in 1932 while visiting the Daly River in the Northern Territory.

of command' from 'a secret wisdom, a power, and a dream shared by no one else on the Daly River'.[14]

Stanner's most important writing as an anthropologist was the book *On Aboriginal Religion*.[15] In another essay titled 'Some Aspects of Aboriginal Religion', he wrote that 'only a blindness of the mind's eye prevented Europeans in the past from seeing that "the ritual uses of water, blood, earth and other substances, in combination with words, gestures, chants, songs and dances, all having for the Aborigines a compelling quality" were not "mere barbarisms" but had a sacramental quality', and that:

> 'one doubts if anywhere could be found more vivid illustrations of a belief in spiritual power laying hold of material things and ennobling them under a timeless purpose in which men feel they have a place.' Obviously, one has to look beyond the symbols to what is symbolised; behind the spoken images of myth, the acted images and gestures of rite, and the graven or painted images of art, to what they stand for; beyond the chrism of blood and ochre to what they point to, with the Aboriginal *Weltanschauung* [worldview].[16]

Durmugam taught Stanner about what should be held most dear, even in the darkest times: the value of a person's life is in *how* it is lived.

Imagine my excitement when, one morning at the Yuendumu Sports Carnival, I woke to see one of these famous ritual duels – what the Yolŋu people call a makarrat̲a – as described by earlier anthropologists such as Stanner and Donald Thomson.[17] I observed from my swag, on a ridge above the flat ground, an old man singing loudly and shaking a bundle of spears, stepping decisively and slowly towards a younger man. Men had gathered around each of them and there was a buzz of tense mumbling. The old man began to throw his spears, one by one, at the younger man, who ducked and weaved as they flew at him.

As I observed many years ago, these duel-like events provided an opportunity for men with very serious grievances against another to call their accusers to account. Few other matters 'led to the level of dispute that marriage negotiations caused', alongside marital infidelity and 'wife-stealing'.[18] I came to understand that while these spectacular scenes grabbed the attention of observers, the mainstays of Aboriginal law were more mundane, entangled in complex kinship and descent relationships, affiliations to land and water, and ceremonial observance.

These laws are not easily understood, which partly explains why the British legal system denied their existence, and continues to do so in several ways. But exist they do. I learnt about them by being involved in events, by being there when it happened, when disputes broke out, when people died, when babies were born, and when people, including myself, broke laws. I once lay down from exhaustion on the ground during a funeral ceremony in northern Australia and was roundly admonished. On another occasion, I spoke to a person who, as it turned out, was my 'poison cousin', and was told to turn around and look the other way. I came to understand that there are many of these subtle rules in a larger body of laws of a sacred and esoteric nature.

This extraordinary event, and my many other encounters with Indigenous laws, confirmed for me what elders like Koiki Mabo had imagined: that our laws could be recognised as legitimate and relevant in contemporary Australia and coexist with the laws that the British had brought. I longed to write about this, and did so in my doctoral thesis. One of my supervisors was Nancy Williams, whose 1986 book *The Yolŋu and Their Land* also confirmed for me that Indigenous laws were a great treasure of wisdom and traditions that served to enhance the lives of people who followed them. Property laws are just one aspect of these elaborate legal systems. Writing on her approach to understanding the Yolŋu land tenure system of north-east Arnhem Land, Williams stated:

> The Yolŋu system of land tenure is one of jural principles that define interests in land as property, rights which are sanctioned ultimately by religion. I wanted to show how Yolŋu derive from those principles a set of relationships that define rights of ownership, rights of use, and rights of succession, and the rules that define persons in whom these various categories of rights are vested … I wanted to show how people can operate within this framework of law to enjoy rights, to exercise power, and extend influence; how their political organisation entails structures of governance embedded in relations to land through which control is legitimately exercised, and how people may seek to redefine these relations to their advantage.[19]

This desire for an understanding of, and respect for, our laws can be found throughout the many petitions written by Aboriginal people and delivered to governors, parliaments, the British Crown, and the Australian people. The survivors of the Tasmanian genocide from Ben Lomond and Big River, and those western communities who had been incarcerated on Flinders Island under false pretences by George Augustus Robinson, wrote letters objecting to the cruel conditions they suffered. As Ann Curthoys and Jessie Mitchell have noted, as early as 1846, Indigenous residents 'drew up the first petition to a reigning monarch from an Aboriginal group in the Australian colonies.' To no avail.[20] Many more letters, petitions and statements have followed in the two centuries since then. While most resulted in cold disdain and contempt, a few have removed the foot of the oppressor from our heads ever so slightly.

The Uluru Statement from the Heart was issued as an outcome of a historic gathering of more than 250 Aboriginal and Torres Strait Islander people at the First Nations National Constitutional Convention in 2017. It calls for the 'establishment of a First Nations Voice enshrined in the Constitution'.[21] The coexistence of ancient and pre-existing Indigenous polities or nations with the Commonwealth of Australia, and the ethical basis for their future recognition by formal constitutional or legislative means, is a matter that is close to the hearts of most Aboriginal and Torres Strait Islander people. Sovereignty, as I see it, is the legal personality of Indigenous polity and a social complex that is at once deeply emotional, social and political.

It seems to me that the concept of sovereignty developed in the Western legal tradition to describe nation states is artificial if applied to the Indigenous relationship to land that lies at the core of our legal systems. A more appropriate concept is reflected in the opinion of Judge Fouad Ammoun of the International Court of Justice in 1975 in the Western Sahara case.[22] During this case, Congolese jurist Nicolas Bayona Ba Meya dismissed the materialistic concept of terra nullius that had led to the dismemberment of Africa following the Berlin Conference of 1884–85. He substituted for this 'a spiritual notion: the ancestral tie between the land, or "mother nature", and the man who was born therefrom remains attached thereto, and must one day return thither to be united with his ancestors'.[23]

This link is the basis of the ownership of the soil or, better, sovereignty of the kind that Indigenous Australians mean when they refer to their spiritual affiliations to land and waters.[24] It is this attachment to places through ancestors and tradition that enables us, as Indigenous people, to claim a kind of sovereignty in Australia that pre-dates the British Crown, and to have a sense of place that is, again, at once deeply emotional, social and political.

It is by following the laws and ways of the ancestors that these affiliations, now recognised by the High Court of Australia as native title, have been transmitted to us today over countless generations. Such a subtle body of laws has not been easy for Australian courts and their British legal traditions to recognise. Yet more than 200 years after the arrival of the British in Australia, our legal traditions still run. This is not merely a matter of pride for Indigenous people, it is also fundamental to our sense of self and how we relate to others, and what gives us the will to live and exist.

Back in 2001, I asked:

> So, how can it be explained that native title to land that pre-existed sovereignty and survived has been recognised by the High Court, yet the full body of ancestral Indigenous Australian laws and jurisdiction are deemed by a narrow, historically distorted notion of sovereignty to be incapable of recognition? … I want to argue that it was the failure of colonial governments to make treaties with our ancestors and the subsequent body of justification for that failure, both judicial and political, that deprive Australian Indigenous peoples today of the dignity of exercising fully the

> body of ancestral law in coexistence with the sovereign state. The idea of sovereignty on which this exclusion lies is a fictive account of settlement, a fictive account of dominion and a distortion of more than four centuries of the exercise of sovereignty by the British Crown in the New World.[25]

Two decades later, much has changed, and we know much more about the concept of Indigenous sovereignty as an expression of spiritual affiliation. As law academic Shireen Morris explains in the 2020 *Love v Commonwealth* case,[26] where the right of Indigenous Australians to inalienable citizenship was decided by the High Court of Australia:

> The majority drew upon the common law recognition of native title to acknowledge what Gordon J termed the 'deeper truth' that Indigenous people, as the 'first peoples of this country', carry a unique 'spiritual or metaphysical' connection with the Australian continent.[27]

This connection, the judges wrote, is 'older and deeper than the Constitution' of the Australian Commonwealth.[28] This long-belated recognition of our ancestral laws and their intrinsic nature is a profoundly important basis for understanding Australia for all of its diverse citizens today, and for reimagining the great foundation of our ancient nation as the product of 65,000 years of ancestral endeavours.[29]

Indigenous systems of law are a vital part of Australian life, barely noticed except when litigation is brought to protect our rights.

Even then, the judiciary has failed to understand them, and takes at face value the opinion of 'expert witnesses' – usually White male anthropologists excited by the opportunity to be recorded in the annals of common law. Their opinions have too often wrecked our chances to have our rights recognised or confirmed.

Because so little is understood about our ancient and enduring systems of law, the challenge of explaining them here is profound. I have drawn on the many lessons of being raised as an Aboriginal person, born in the mid-20th century in Queensland, where no civil or human rights were accorded to my people. My personal experiences in everyday life, in land claims and campaigns, lobbying in parliaments, working on inquiries and commissions, and in a government department and universities, have sharpened my sense of the great injustice done to Aboriginal people. My training as a scholar in the humanities, primarily as an anthropologist and geographer, has provided some skills for writing about Aboriginal laws and their resonating presence in Australian society, despite the grand failure to recognise them in large part. I hope I have done justice here to the way of the ancestors.

AARON CORN

Twenty years after Marcia Langton grew up in south-west Queensland, I was raised some 700 kilometres to the east on the Gold Coast in south-east Queensland. Like most young people on the Gold Coast in the 1970s and 1980s, my upbringing was devoid of meaningful exposure to Indigenous Australians and their perspectives.

The entire class time spent on Indigenous topics throughout my school and early university education amounted to only a few hours.

Yet, somehow, the idea of Australia's Indigenous history fascinated me from the age of seven. Driving down the Gold Coast Highway to primary school in the mornings, I went past the Jebribillum Bora Park on the corner of 6th Avenue at Burleigh Heads, which preserves one of the last known original Indigenous ceremony grounds of the local Yugambeh people. I would ask the adults around me inquisitive questions about the site, but their answers were always vague and unsatisfying. So far as I was aware, I did not know any Indigenous people or communities. But why had these people so mysteriously disappeared? Even at that young age, the common explanation that Indigenous people had simply vanished before urbanisation made no sense to me. Four decades later, when three generations of Yugambeh people opened the Gold Coast Commonwealth Games of 2018 with a traditional smoking ceremony, it was plain for all to see that this story had never been true.

Everything changed in the 1990s, when a favourable political climate brought better legal recognition for Indigenous rights in Australia. In 1988, the year of the Australian Bicentenary, the Barunga Statement had called on the Australian Government to make a long-overdue treaty with Indigenous peoples in recognition of their pre-existing sovereignty and human rights, and in 1991 the Parliament of Australia voted unanimously to establish the Council for Aboriginal Reconciliation with a ten-year mandate to consider this prospect. 1n 1992, the High Court of Australia's momentous decision in *Mabo v Queensland (No 2)* overturned the legal doctrine of terra nullius, which the Crown had used to deny Indigenous peoples their rights, and recognised the concept of Indigenous native title under common law. With the Australian Parliament's ensuing passage of the *Native Title Act* in 1993, which was also the International Year for the World's Indigenous People, Australia became a changed nation in which Indigenous native title could legally coexist with Crown title.

At school, I had been very good at music and went on to complete a Bachelor's degree and Honours year at the Queensland Conservatorium, where I mostly played clarinet and studied the canon of Western art music. In 1993, I was offered an opportunity to volunteer as an intern at the Queensland Museum while doing master's research into the large collection of musical instruments there. At the museum, I worked closely with a team of cultural collections curators, including very knowledgeable and approachable Indigenous curators, and found myself handling a diverse array of musical instruments from all over the world, as well as many Indigenous ones from throughout Australia. Realising how very little I knew about those Indigenous instruments and the musicians who had used them, I realised that I had been denied a basic education about my birth country and home.

Also influencing my psyche in the early 1990s was an iconic new Australian band who rapidly rose to stardom and whose music sounded like nothing heard before. Including both Indigenous and other Australian musicians, their name was Yothu Yindi and their music blended Indigenous song styles from Arnhem Land with

Western popular band styles. The lead singer, the late Mandawuy Yunupiŋu (1956–2013), was a Yolŋu man of the Gumatj clan from Yirrkala in north-east Arnhem Land, who had been named the 1992 Australian of the Year; and their most famous song, 'Treaty',[30] called on the Australian Government to fulfil Prime Minister Bob Hawke's promise of a treaty with Indigenous peoples after receiving the Barunga Statement in 1988. I had very little idea of how to understand any of this music or the histories behind it, but could see that this widespread lack of awareness was something that needed to be rectified, particularly given the important perspectives that songs like 'Treaty' intended to share with the broadest audience possible.

When my work at the Queensland Museum wound up, and with very limited guidance and resources, I embarked on a new project as a Doctor of Philosophy student at the University of Melbourne in 1995. I wanted to better understand this new form of musical expression that had been sparked by the burning political issues of Indigenous sovereignty, land rights and treaty-making. This work was very challenging but, as I threw myself into it, I learnt several things very quickly: Australian history was nothing like what I had been taught. Indigenous cultures in Australia and their music were like nothing I had ever imagined. Yothu Yindi and their music were intimately linked to both the Barunga Statement and the preceding three-decade struggle waged by Yolŋu leaders against mining on their homelands. Finally, I learnt that many popular bands had formed in Arnhem Land since the 1960s and performed at annual festivals across the region, helping to develop Yothu Yindi's unique musical style.

Embedded in the lyrics and structures of Yothu Yindi's songs were deliberate pointers to how Mandawuy Yunupiŋu particularly wanted the band's audiences to understand and engage with their music. Their very name describes the *yothu-yindi* relationship between children and their mothers that forms the basis of all functional relationships and legal responsibilities among people and clans in Yolŋu society. Similarly influential was the concept of *ga<u>n</u>ma*, the interaction of freshwater and saltwater currents where creeks meet the coast on the Gumatj homeland of Biranybirany. This stands as a legal template for how different clans should properly form and maintain productive and equitable partnerships. As Yolŋu laws for appropriate relationships between clans, both yothu-yindi and ga<u>n</u>ma model the broader equality and social engagements between Indigenous and other Australians that Yothu Yindi sought to promote through their music and hoped a future treaty would deliver.

I first met Mandawuy Yunupiŋu in Arnhem Land at Gunyaŋara in 1996. I then attended the first Garma Festival, at Gu<u>l</u>ku<u>l</u>a in 1999. It was run by the Yothu Yindi Foundation, which had been set up by the band in 1990 to promote Yolŋu culture and development. In 2002, Mandawuy and I collaborated in running the first Symposium on Indigenous Music and Dance during the Garma Festival, and this led to our creation of the National Recording Project for Indigenous Performance in Australia in 2004. The other founding drivers of these important initiatives, which continue to this day, were Marcia Langton and ethnomusicologist Allan Marett. After I met Marcia at the first Garma Festival, I started working in her Australian Indigenous Studies program at the University of Melbourne in 2001; and after earning my PhD, I went to work for Allan at the University of Sydney in 2004. Our collaborative work from this period continues to be influential and, in 2020, led to the creation of the International Council for Traditional Music (ICTM) Study Group on Indigenous Music and Dance, with Marcia as its inaugural Chair.[31]

My 2009 book on Yothu Yindi, *Reflections & Voices*, puts forward many of Mandawuy Yunupiŋu's unfiltered views on the presence and practice of Indigenous laws and leadership in contemporary Australia, including a full transcript of our keynote interview for the Music and Social Justice Conference at the University of Sydney in 2005.[32] In that interview, I asked Mandawuy if he agreed with the notion that every time someone sings or dances in ceremony, they are actively maintaining sovereign relationships to country in Australia that pre-date the British Crown. Without hesitation, he responded:

> Very much so, many people would agree with that, because we're still practising our law. We're still doing it regardless of our laws being rejected or being trivialised by mainstream Australian law. We don't care. We keep going, because it's important to pass our law on to the next generation. It strengthens our identity as Aboriginal people, the First Nations of this country.[33]

While Yothu Yindi taught me to see the presence and practice of Indigenous laws and leadership in contemporary Australia, it was another Yolŋu mentor who taught me how to understand the finer workings of Indigenous laws and leadership structures.

The late Joe Neparrŋa Gumbula (1954–2015) was a leader of the Gupapuyŋu clan. Born into a long line of Yolŋu leaders at Miliŋinbi (Milingimbi) in Arnhem Land, he moved to the neighbouring town of Galiwin'ku as a teenager and in 1971 joined the legendary local band Soft Sands as a singer and guitarist. Leaving school at the age of sixteen, he apprenticed as a carpenter and would later have a career as a sworn officer in the Northern Territory Police. He simultaneously trained to qualify as a *d̲alkarramirri* (powerful) leader, selected and authorised by elders to practise Yolŋu law via the comprehensive planning and direction of large groups of performers and artisans in complex public ceremonies. This long and arduous process entails many years of diligent study and practice, as well as an ability to master, perform and combine all song, dance and design parts of public ceremonies in their entirety.

Having been invited to a festival at Galiwin'ku by Soft Sands, I first met Joe in 1997, the year he was made d̲alkarramirri after retiring from the Northern Territory Police. While I was focused on Soft Sands' music at the time, Joe's interest in me, as a young music student with good research skills, ran far deeper than I could have imagined. Since retiring from the police, he had become passionate about locating and gathering the substantial records of his family's history at Miliŋinbi since the 1920s that were held in museums and other collections worldwide. He had already retrieved a copy of a 1964 film by the Australian Institute of Aboriginal and Torres Strait Islander Studies (AIATSIS) in Canberra that documented his father leading a public ceremony at Miliŋinbi,[34] and had worked material from it into a new music video for his own original song 'Djiliwirri'.[35] But he had no intention of stopping there.

The deal Joe initially put to me was fair, balanced and straightforward: he would teach me about Yolŋu music and law, and I would work for him to locate and access collections of interest around the world. At that moment, he and I became *bäpa'manydji*: teacher-and-student, master-and-apprentice or, as Yolŋu people usually describe it, father-and-child. Charming yet uncompromising, Joe expected me to take our relationship extremely seriously. Once, early on, he furiously chided me for not grasping that, from a Yolŋu perspective, adoptive relationships are very real. My naive misunderstanding that they were not provoked such great offence and anger in Joe that I never made that mistake again.

Ultimately, Joe Gumbula shaped my thinking and approaches in ways that no other teacher could. In our formal portrait from my PhD graduation at the University of Melbourne in 2003, his fatherly hand rests on my shoulder. He encouraged me to take public ceremonies seriously and dance whenever he sang for them. Post-graduation, he began teaching me his traditional songs, primarily so I could play *yiḏaki* (didjeridu) to accompany him singing whenever we travelled together. He constantly drew on his song knowledge to teach me about Yolŋu law. When we began co-writing academic publications at this time, our aim was *not* to bring Yolŋu knowledge into universities but, rather, to bring universities into more equitable dialogues with Yolŋu leaders. We conceived of our approach as being not only bicultural, but also 'bi-intellectual'.[36] In 2006, we had planned to write a book together on key concepts in Yolŋu culture, but were unable to find a mature enough publisher for it at the time. Many of the concepts we had long discussed are now addressed in this book and stand as a fitting tribute to Joe's extraordinary teachings and intellectual contributions.

Joe and I would work together and help each other grow our careers at the University of Melbourne, University of Sydney and Australian National University for eighteen years in total. In 2007, his groundbreaking work led him to become the first Yolŋu person to be awarded a project grant by the Australian Research Council (ARC). In the same year, his academic contributions and achievements were further recognised when the University of Sydney awarded him with an honorary Doctor of Music.

Inspired by these successes, I later collaborated in similar collections work with the Warlpiri leader Steven Wantarri 'Wanta' Jampijinpa Pawu from Lajamanu. In 2005, Wanta founded and was Creative Director of the Milpirri Festival at Lajamanu, which was built on his philosophy of *ngurra-kurlu* (home-having) and its five fundamental principles of *jaru* (language), *warlalja* (kin), *kuruwarru* (law), *manyuwana* (ceremony) and *walya* (land).[37] In 2012, Wanta became the first Warlpiri person to be awarded an ARC project grant.

I went to work at the Centre for Aboriginal Studies in Music at the University of Adelaide in 2016 before returning to the University of Melbourne in 2020, where I now work in the Indigenous Knowledge Institute alongside many talented colleagues from Indigenous and other backgrounds. They include three outstanding Indigenous leaders who became our inaugural Professorial

Fellows: Diane Kerr, a Woiwurrung Wurundjeri traditional owner of Melbourne; Brian Djangirrawuy Gumbula-Garawirrtja, who continues the work of Joe Gumbula; and Wanta Pawu.[38]

Today, Joe's professional legacy endures through the ongoing work of the many collections managers and researchers he so generously mentored. His painted diagram of the *Yolŋu Knowledge Constitution*, created in 2002, continues to serve as an informative guide to the structure of the Yolŋu legal system and traditional definitions of access to hereditary knowledge and resources. Sources like this, and Wanta's philosophy of ngurra-kurlu, offer important guidelines for understanding how Indigenous laws and leadership structures operate in Australia, and what aspects of them can be disclosed in public settings.

Restrictions on what information can be shared in public, particularly where private and sensitive matters are concerned, exist in all human societies, and Indigenous societies in Australia are no different. Joe's and Wanta's models address the totality of their respective Yolŋu and Warlpiri legal structures without disclosing any restricted information, while simultaneously showing how their respective societies train and authorise leaders who are qualified to deal with such matters. These structures, as outlined, for example, by Yolŋu leaders in the Elcho Island and Yirrkala Petitions of 1998 (see Chapter 4), are vital to understanding how Indigenous legal systems endure in Australia and how they can hold relevance for everyone amid present-day efforts to finally realise a treaty with Indigenous Australians.

Beyond this immediate concern, however, many Indigenous leaders passionately agree that the values and insights offered by their laws for living a good life can hold potential benefits for everyone. Everything that Indigenous leaders have ever told me about their laws has been shared with the intent of making the world a better place. Evidence for this lies everywhere. Thoughtful and generous leaders such as Paul Gordon and Paul Callaghan, for example, have adapted wisdom shared from their respective Ngiyampaa and Warrimay backgrounds to help broader audiences find meaning in the contemporary world.[39] Marcia Langton has initiated the Ngarrnga Aboriginal and Torres Strait Islander Curricula Project because of her firm conviction that 'Every Australian student is entitled to know the truth about their country'.[40] Meanwhile, ranger programs directed by a multitude of Indigenous leaders Australia-wide work ceaselessly to care for their homelands and combat the worst impacts of climate change for us all.

I thank all such Indigenous leaders for so generously sharing their wisdom and vision, and hope this book makes a positive contribution to broadening understanding of their important teachings.

2

FIRST LAW

Daymbalipu Munuŋgurr was a powerful Yolŋu clan leader from north-east Arnhem Land who lived in the community of Yirrkala when Marcia Langton first met him in 1989. Marcia's friend Evelyn Schaber offered to introduce her, made the appointment with him, and instructed her on how to approach him. She told her to sit on the ground in front of him and tell him her name and why she wanted to see him.

The day was a typical sunny, clear day on the northern coastline in the dry season, and Munuŋgurr was sitting on a white plastic chair under a tree. He held a staff as a sign of his authority. Langton walked over, sat in front of him and outlined the work she was undertaking for the Royal Commission into Aboriginal Deaths in Custody to investigate twelve cases of Indigenous men who had died in prisons and police custody in the Northern Territory.

Munuŋgurr described how hard drugs and alcohol had been introduced to the Yolŋu homelands after the construction of the local bauxite mine in 1968, which brought an influx of more than 1000 miners and their families. He explained how this had disrupted Yolŋu community life and disoriented young people to the extent that they began failing to follow law and behave appropriately at ceremonies. Alcohol became readily available when the Walkabout Hotel opened in nearby Nhulunbuy in 1971. Its immediate effect was disastrous. People living traditionally in the remote homelands surrounding Yirrkala likened the epidemic of illness and death from alcohol to a catastrophic sorcery attack. The dangerous health risks to young people of sniffing petrol, including brain damage, were also a major concern. Munuŋgurr's assessment of this disaster as a senior Yolŋu leader was stern.

After more than an hour of discussion, Marcia took the key lessons from Munuŋgurr that culture is law and that people and societies cannot function properly without it:

> Culture fading away slowly. So many people think they're White these days, especially young people.
>
> Yeah, culture broken down. *Yo* [Yes], they running away from ceremony, because of *ŋänitji* [alcohol]. Young children, school age, they got to learn their culture. But middle-age boy and girl, they want to run away to the parks. They come back really drunk, fussing about, you know. In the ceremony, they fighting and talking wrong time – too fussy.

> When they sober, like we today, we never be break up culture. When that happening, drinking business, they break and kick the culture. When people are making ceremony, you know, then they come in and disturbing our ceremony and culture.
>
> So, they are not worrying about their cultural things, but only ŋänitji.
>
> Yo, yo, but if they were sober, they would have respect.
>
> Respect, yo, yo. Only when they are drinking, young people speaking bad words, swearing *Balanda* [English] words at the old men. They know all the Balanda swear words when they are drunk.[1]

More than three decades later, it is clear that Munuŋgurr's concerns were prescient. He understood the impact of alcohol in north-east Arnhem Land and worked hard with anthropologists such as Janice Reid and Nancy Williams to document the frightening increase in mortality that followed its introduction at the Walkabout Hotel. Their findings were published in the *Medical Journal of Australia*.[2] He also recorded hundreds of hours of his own ceremonial singing on audiotape, hoping that he could hold back the tide of cultural destruction. This approach was largely successful, and his work is acknowledged by a room named in his honour at AIATSIS in Canberra.

Munuŋgurr was a great Yolŋu law man who was dedicated to preserving his law, as so many elders of his generation were. His concern was the transmission of ceremonial knowledge and experiences to younger people, because it is by attending ceremonies that people can learn law and find meaning and purpose in themselves and their lives. He knew that without law, we are lost.

HOLDING LAW

All human cultures have systems of law designed to help societies function and maintain standards of living. Ancient sites and artefacts show us that humans have lived in Australia for at least 65,000 years, which pre-dates the human settlement of Europe and the Americas. Over this immense stretch of time, Indigenous groups across Australia developed complex systems of law that enabled people to live in a wide variety of natural environments and changing climatic conditions. Indigenous systems of law carry countless generations of knowledge. Without law, the ancestors who arrived, travelled and created human societies here would not have survived and thrived over more than sixty-five millennia. These societies changed over time but were able to continue through major climatic changes, such as the last Ice Age peak around 20,000 years ago and the last major sea-level rise some 10,000 years ago.

Human history in Australia, then, began more than 65,000 years before the British started to colonise this continent in 1788. Over those long millennia, Indigenous peoples of Australia came to value the keeping of law as the most significant endeavour in life. Following law in Indigenous societies is the most important and time-honoured way of living. Through law, people express their humanity, honour their ancestors, care for their homelands and environments, understand the past and present, build families and communities, grow in wisdom, and plan for the future.

In Indigenous languages of Australia, common words for 'law' mean precisely what they mean in English, and more. Fundamentally, law is a system of rules created and observed within societies to instil people with good values and encourage beneficial behaviours. However, common words for 'law' in Indigenous languages, such as *rom* in the Yolŋu languages, hold broader meanings than 'law' does in English. The idea of law in Indigenous societies, while remaining a system of rules for social good, also includes the idea of the English word 'culture'. Beyond this, it also captures the idea of 'proper practice' – the correct way of living a good life, as passed down from ancestors over many generations – and the idea of 'the way': the path through life shown by ancestors who have gone before. While some Indigenous people today prefer to use the homophone 'lore' to distinguish their ways from Western law, these complementary definitions traditionally work together in harmony to imbue law with an additional sense of the cultural and the sacred. Keeping law is about more than just following rules – it is a way of living that honours the sacred relationships Indigenous people hold with their ancestors and homelands.

This may give the impression that Indigenous cultures in Australia are static and unchanging, but that is far from true. Indigenous cultures were able to accommodate new ideas, technologies and innovations long before the arrival of the British First Fleet at Sydney Cove in 1788. This is evident, for example, in the history of international trade along the northern coastlines of the continent. Indigenous groups in the Kimberley region of Western Australia and Arnhem Land in the Northern Territory were engaged in trade with merchant fleets from Makassar on the Indonesian island of Sulawesi, as well as other foreign seafarers from the north, long before the arrival of the British. Indigenous bodies of law in these regions record rich histories of foreign exchange and detail the new kinds of goods and technologies that Makassans and other seafarers traded into north Australia, including exotic cloth and metal items, and foods such as rice.

Law, then, is constantly evolving in response to new needs and circumstances. It emphasises continuity with the ancestral past as the sacred bond that links people to their homelands, but offers each new generation the possibility of adding their own understandings and innovations to the ancestral store of knowledge. In the Yolŋu languages, babies are said to crawl with law (*rom-gal'-gal'maranhamirri*). They are born with law as an innately human trait and learn law from birth. All Yolŋu people are considered to be *rom-waṯaŋu* (law-holding), while very kind and giving people are said to be *rom-djägamirri* (law-caring).

Law sets a basic standard for acceptable behaviours in Indigenous societies, as well as high learning standards for educating leaders in society. When law functions properly, it creates optimal conditions for maintaining peace and stability. In every society, though, there are those who breach laws, and for them there are legal penalties ranging from social and physical isolation to corporal and capital punishments. The potential to break the law is recognised in Indigenous culture as a common trait, and this acknowledgement leaves everyone with a choice about how they will act in relation to others and in the world. Many of the ancestral stories that convey the origins of Indigenous laws tell us about how ancestral beings broke laws, killed people, stole wives, ignored their children, stole food, committed adultery and behaved badly in myriad other ways. Their fates are often terrifying: they continue to live in the eternal 'everywhen' in rocks or underground, or are victims of vengeance.[3] Other stories tell us about ancestral beings that took the form of animals, and their adventures in dramatically different environments than those familiar to us. Their behaviour gives hints about the species whose form they took, and infer rules for engaging with them with respect.

These stories from a sacred past are more than parables, more than narratives, and more than morality tales. They hold a form of knowledge that is called law. The law-giving ancestral beings are ever-present. How we live our lives among them is enhanced by observing the law.

THE OLD PEOPLE

When the first ancestors of humans arrived as creator beings in Australia, they found the continent featureless and unformed. At the places where they landed from the ocean or the sky, their arrival marked the landscape and formed geographical features such as cliffsides and mountains. These foundational sites of ancestral arrival are dotted all over the Australian continent and are considered to be the most important of ancestral places.

The original ancestral beings took many forms and are often said to have been able to change their appearance. Many had human forms while also being able to assume the forms of a variety of other animal species. This is why so many Indigenous people today say that their original ancestors were not human but supra-human. If a homeland was founded by a Shark ancestor of any given species, for example, then that country and its traditional owners remain Shark to this day, as do all their associated laws and ceremonies. This is because, as each original ancestor founded a new homeland around the foundation site where it first landed, it marked and entered the land, describing all its features and species with a unique set of sacred names as it went, imbuing it for all time with the sacred gift of life.

In Indigenous law, these original ancestors are viewed as eternal. Their arrivals happened so exceedingly long ago that they are considered to have taken place before time and the seasons began. They founded an ornate patchwork of myriad different countries across Australia as homes for the many diverse groups of their descent, and created waterways and overland routes across vast distances that connected these peoples through trade. Their patchwork of different homelands remains today, stretching across Australia's remotest regions to the centres of its cities.

While the seasons and other natural cycles regulate life in the physical world, the original ancestors are said to remain eternal. They are ever-present and ever-knowing in country, ready to help their living descendants and repel unwanted intruders. The aim of law and ceremonies is, therefore, to maintain peace and order across the whole of reality by keeping all life in our physical world in mirrored balance with the original ancestors' presence.

While ever-present in the physical world, the original ancestors are also said to remain anchored in the eternal metaphysical domains from which they initially came. Sometimes these homes are said to be the Milky Way in the night sky, or beyond the horizon across the ocean. This introduces the idea of the 'dreaming', both as an ancient time when the first ancestors arrived and interacted with the first humans, and as an eternal realm that remains linked to the physical world today through humanity's sacred bond with ancestors.

Coinage of the term 'dreaming' in English came through FJ Gillen's ethnographic research among desert groups in Central Australia in the late 19th century. He translated the Arrernte word *altyerrenge*, from the root word *altyerre* (dream), as 'the dream times'.[4] Later, in the mid 20th century, the anthropologist WEH Stanner offered 'the dreaming' as a better approximation, arguing that:

> Comparable terms from other tribes [groups] are often almost untranslatable or mean literally something like 'men of old [old people]'. Some anthropologists have called it the Eternal Dream Time. I prefer to call it what many Aborigines call it in English: The Dreaming, or just, Dreaming.
>
> A central meaning of The Dreaming is that of a sacred, heroic time long ago when man and nature came to be as they are; but neither 'time' nor 'history' as we understand them is involved in this meaning.
>
> A blackfellow [Indigenous person] may call his totem [ancestor], or the place from which his spirit came, his Dreaming. He may also explain the existence of a custom, or law of life, as causally due to The Dreaming ...
>
> Although ... The Dreaming conjures up the notion of a sacred, heroic time of the indefinitely remote past, such a time

> is also, in a sense, still part of the present. One cannot 'fix' The Dreaming *in* time: it was, and is, everywhen ... [and] has ... an unchallengeably sacred authority.
>
> ... The Dreaming is many things in one. Among them, a kind of narrative of things that once happened; a kind of charter of things that still happen; and a kind of *logos* or principle of order transcending everything significant for Aboriginal man [*sic*]. If I am correct in saying so, it is much more complex philosophically than we have so far realised ...
>
> Why the blackfellow thinks of 'dreaming' as the nearest equivalent in English is a puzzle. It may be because it is by the act of dreaming, as reality and symbol, that the Aboriginal mind makes contact – thinks it makes contact – with whatever mystery it is that connects The Dreaming and the Here-and-Now.[5]

Due to these writers, 'dreaming' is now used generically in English to describe Indigenous spirituality and ancestral law across all Aboriginal groups. But the term is most closely aligned with desert law. In the Warlpiri language of the Tanami Desert, for example, *jukurr-mani* means 'dream', while *jukurrpa* can also be translated as 'dreaming'. This is not a universal rule, however, and 'dreaming' does not accurately reflect how all Indigenous languages express ideas about ancestral law and spirituality. For that matter, the anthropological term 'totem' is also highly inaccurate and better avoided.

In the Yolŋu languages, for example, *waŋarr* is the term used to describe both the first ancestors who came long ago (*baman'*) and all ancestors from whom people today are descended. The term 'old people' when used in English can refer to both kinds of ancestors, who are ultimately one and the same. The term 'rom' refers to the body of ancestral laws handed down from the original ancestors over countless generations, while the term *maḏayin,* which is also exceedingly difficult to translate into English, describes the deep sacredness of the natural beauty that the original ancestors instilled in the physical world. The neighbouring Anindilyakwa language of Arnhem Land's eastern islands holds yet another way of understanding the eternal influence of ancestral law upon all life and things in the physical world:

> 'In the beginning, now and forever more', is *Amawurrena–alawudawarra. Amawurrena–alawudawarra* can best be translated ... as 'Creation–substance power'. *Amawurrena* is the passive aspect, *alawudawarra* the active. Implicit within it (if indeed it is an 'it') are differentiated, archetypal Forms which, in the beginning of Creation, remained silent and unincarnated. Then these Forms began to sound and become visible, moving in waves of varying shapes and shaping the spiritual substances through which they moved.
>
> The enFormed substances then began to solidify into more precisely defined shapes (supra-natural Beings or 'Dreamings'); and finally incarnated as landForms, natural speciesForms, and humanForms ... Though these material entities incarnate, pass away, and incarnate again over time on 'this side [the physical world]', their source, *Amawurrena–alawudawarra* in its manifold

Forms, continues to exist as an eternal present not only on the 'other side' but also as an enForming Presence on 'this side' (*awarrawalya* ...).

In other words, the eternal Formations *extend through* from the 'other side' to 'this side' to bridge the two dimensions of reality. From within the Formations on the 'other side', individual bits of Creation-substance are 'expelled' across to 'this side' to animate or inForm the individual material incarnations that are constantly appearing through the productive process. Each person/species (and inanimate object during the initial phases of its incarnation), is ... enFormed by archetypal spirit and inFormed by a personal spirit *(amugwa)*. When the material body dies, your personal spirit returns to the 'other side' along the archetypal enFormation or 'pathway' through which it entered the world, perhaps to reincarnate at a later date ...

On the 'other side' these enFormations are in constant motion while you, your inner spirit, remains in place ... On 'this side', by contrast, the enFormations assume a fixed position, 'bounding' land, natural species, and humans. Existence as a whole, then, is rather like a rubber band passing through a waterfall ... stretched to its limit and then rotated from one side ... through to the other. Each of us comes across to 'this side' at birth, is Formally embodied, lives, dies, and then returns to a fixed position on the 'other side'. Both 'sides', then, exist side-by-side in mirrored image ... The purpose of life on 'this side' ... is not only to realise the nature of the 'other side' while you are here, but also to bring life on 'this side' into mirrored concert with it.[6]

To put it simply, if the original ancestor who founded your homeland took a shark of any given species as its primary form, you would be a Shark person and, depending on how inheritance law primarily flows in your part of Australia, all direct ancestors in your female or male lineage would also have been Shark people. Through that direct lineage, your main homeland would be Shark country and all ceremonies held by people in that lineage would be under the original Shark ancestor's law. Knowledge of how that same shark species appears and behaves in nature would inform how you read the features and conditions of your main homeland, as well as the processes of everyday activities, such as hunting, and ceremonies performed by people who share in that Shark ancestry with you. This is how the Shark people to whom you belong care for your homeland and honour your ancestors, so that seasons and life cycles in the physical world remain in mirrored concert with the Shark ancestor's eternal ancestral domain. For you, this law provides the way shown by ancestors for navigating life and potentially growing enough in wisdom over decades to eventually add your own unique contributions and perspectives to this ancestral store of Shark knowledge.

THE SPEAKING HOMELANDS

Places where ancestors are 'sleeping' are prominent features in Indigenous law. A relationship between a person and a place is fundamental in Indigenous law because living people share a spiritual substance with these ancestors. Stanner was among the first of many anthropologists who attempted to explain this phenomenon, describing the sharing of spiritual substance among persons, places and ancestral beings as the 'everywhen'.[7] Anthropologists RM Berndt and CH Berndt used the term 'speaking land' to convey a sense of dialogue in Indigenous relationships with the natural environment and ancestors,[8] while Nancy Munn, who worked with Warlpiri people, was the first to use the term 'consubstantiality' to convey the eternal influence of ancestors upon the physical world.[9] Nancy Williams has used the term 'sentient landscapes' to describe how Indigenous people view their landscapes as responsive, communicative and conscious.[10]

This sense of living in coexistent relationships with other species and ancestors is rich with significance and meaning to Indigenous people, irrespective of whether they are now traditional owners of a remote homeland or a major city. Places have their own agency. They speak, and the ancestral beings within them are agents in the spiritual encounters that living people have with them. Typically, it is tradition for senior Indigenous people to call out to their ancestors and speak to them. Places have an energetic presence that holds all manner of information available to traditional owners, especially elders. Knowledgeable elders have relationships with special places that are imbued with remembered qualities. These include their spiritual significance, geographic and ecological features, food and medicinal resources, physical and spiritual dangers, and presence in personal memories and stories. Sometimes the most protected and sacred places in Indigenous laws and ceremonies are essential to sustaining drinkable water sources and food security overall, and also to enhancing the likelihood of increasing those water sources and boosting food security. Physical features of lands and waters are not merely places but, along with their physical and environmental characteristics, carry evidence of spiritual events involving the original ancestors whose powers persist.

Senior traditional owners typically work hard throughout their lives to gain and hold intimate knowledge of their homelands and all their physical features and sacred connections. This is a necessary part of their inherited entitlement to those places. Such elders are also mindful of their group's territorial boundaries and the interests of relatives from other places through shared family lineages. Speaking the specific language of a place and holding the unique set of sacred names given to a distinct homeland, as given by the ancestral beings residing in it, are constant reminders of these property relations. From cities to remote homelands across Australia, 'naming ceremonies' bind a person's identity to a place with the conferral of a sacred name linked to it. Travelling across the land to hunt, fish, and harvest other foods and resources reminds people of events in each place and how the features and movements of all species, waters, celestial bodies and weather phenomena – from birds and fish to rainbows and sunsets – are recorded and held as sacred in ancestral law.

Throughout Australia, people use fire to burn country as a means of ecological management and conservation to regenerate fire-dependent trees and vegetation. This seasonal burning of landscapes is an important way of practising law that encourages new shoots to spring up from the plants' roots.

While rare today, women's practice of giving birth at trees and memorialising them as 'birthing trees' stands as another example of how places and species are entwined with ancestral law. Most Indigenous groups have sacred traditional beliefs about the consubstantiality of people, places and ancestors, and their connections across all eternity. This way of thinking about the meaning and significance of places and their connections to people through ancestral law is a toolbox for interpreting landscapes, both familiar and newly encountered. In writing about the Pama people of Cape York in north Queensland, linguistic anthropologist Bruce Rigsby best summarised this way of thinking about our place in the world:

> In the first instance, the Pama belong to the land because they share a spiritual essence in common with it ... but Pama children are not simply made up from flesh and blood. All Pama have a spirit counterpart or alter ego, which comes from the land and from the Old People. That is, a person's spirit does not come into existence from nothing, but it comes from spirit that has always existed in and on the land, and it enters the embryo at or sometime after conception. Moreover, a person's spirit does not just come from anywhere; it comes from [an individuated Story-Being inhabiting] a specific country or place. In this way, each Pama person incarnates a spirit that indissolubly connects them with a country of origin ...
>
> That is why we say that the Pama belong to the land. They are a part of the land just as a person's head is a part of their body. The late Professor Stanner spoke of this relationship as one *in animam*

'in spirit.'[11] It is a spiritual relationship because spirit connects people to their land. Linguists would describe it as a relationship of inalienable possession, the relationship of a part to its whole.

Pama also have a material relationship to the land. It is a relationship *in rem* 'in a thing'. People's rights *in rem* to country derive from their spiritual relationship to it *in animam* and depend upon it. This provides the root of their traditional title to land. There were no written title deeds to record that so-and-so acquired such-and-such land by purchase or grant of the Crown. Instead, Pama know and tell how the Stories fashioned a specific landscape and in a number of locations 'sat down' there to remain for all time ... Their title derives from the creative acts of the ancestral Stories in the Story-Time and from the unbroken links of spirit among the land, their Old People and themselves. Pama people also say that it was not just during the Story-Time that the Stories lived and acted. They still live in and on the land, as do the spirits of the Old People, the long dead and recently dead alike.

This is why we say that the land belongs to the Pama. They own the land; that is, they have rights *in rem* to the land and the sea. Phrased differently, we can say that specific groups of people have specific rights in specific tracts of land 'as against the world'. These include rights to live on the land, to use and enjoy it in various ways, to speak of and present themselves as its owners and to exclude others in various ways from exercising the same rights. Linguists would describe this as a relationship of alienable possession, the culturally constituted and socially sanctioned relationship which we conventionally call 'ownership'.[12]

An example of reading a place encountered for the first time is described by the anthropologist Howard Morphy when he accompanied a famous Yolŋu painter from northern Australia, Narritjin Maymuru, to the Snowy Mountains in south-eastern Australia.[13] This senior Indigenous man recognised that the place they were visiting was connected to his own Yolŋu law, even though he had never been there before and it was more than 2000 kilometres from his homeland. Morphy noted that 'One of the significant things about what I would term Narritjin's "reinterpretation" of the Snowy Mountains landscape is that for him it was not a reinterpretation but a process of discovery or revelation'.[14] Narritjin told Morphy how the Snowy Mountains' natural features reminded him of his own country and its ancestral and ceremonial links to ancestral law.

> I asked Narritjin how he knew ... since neither of us had ever been there before. Moreover, little was known of the mythology of the people who had once lived in the area before their lives had been so rudely interrupted by European colonization in the middle of the last century. Narritjin pointed to the sharp pebbles that lay beside the stream that were Ganydjalala's stone spears, and he pointed out the trees that were similar to those in the forests through which Ganydjalala hunted, and finally he reminded me of how the lake she created was represented in paintings on the djuwany posts made for the Djuŋuwan ceremony by his brother Bokarra, and how its shape resembled the shape of the lake by which we were sitting.[15]

Along with descent from the original ancestors, it is also commonly believed in Indigenous societies that babies are conceived as spiritual beings. Conception and the beginning of a baby's life are primarily linked to the entry of an ancestral spirit into the mother. Put another way, people are conceived as spiritual beings who are brought into existence by their ancestors, the old people. A person's spiritual being is also grounded in specific places: the homelands where they are perceived or remembered to have been conceived, been born, lived, died and anchored eternally to their original ancestors. Their spiritual significance infuses all ceremonial practices and everyday experiences with a special, ancestral sense of place that is mediated by elders through the observance of ancestral law in ceremonies. Here, the ancestral connections of places are expressed through unique sets of names, songs, dances and designs that were created by the original ancestors when they first observed the homelands they shaped into homes for people of their descent. Guided by elders and qualified ceremonial leaders, these expressions enliven places with sacred power and awaken the ancestors who reside within them in familiar ways. While the original ancestors and the dead can be a great danger to intruders, performing ceremonies in the correct way with familiar songs, dances and designs consistent with ancestral law can render potentially dangerous places welcoming and bountiful. Indeed, when Indigenous people welcome newcomers to their country, it is this kind of ancestral permission and protection that is sought for all parties.

SYSTEMS OF LAW

Indigenous law traditions vary across regions, with major and minor differences between even closely neighbouring peoples. These variations are highly valued because they are markers of differentiation among the hundreds of distinct Indigenous peoples across Australia. While these differences have been explained as resulting from ecological variations across different regions, there is much more to the ways their respective bodies of law are expressed through different genres of ceremonial practice. These regional systems of law are centred around major ancestors and ancestral events and tell us about especially important laws and how people are connected across vast landscapes. Big ceremonial alliances draw law men and law women together through extensive family networks. The recent history of one regional system of law helps to illustrate this.

In the Kimberley region of northern Western Australia, the *wirnan*, sometimes spelt *wurnan* or *wunan*, is a ritual trading cycle that began with the ancestors of the sacred past. On Karunjie Station in the East Kimberley, successive generations of Ngarinyin people 'have maintained and adapted the two very different systems of wirnan and the pastoral station economy within their social worlds'.[16] Anthropologist Anthony Redmond and historian Fiona Skyring write:

> The traditional *Wurnan* trade network spans a number of socio-cultural regions in the Kimberley region of Western Australia and beyond, operating at both small-scale interpersonal and larger-scale

> inter-group levels, channelling ritual and simple economic objects of desire through predetermined but flexible trading routes.[17]

For more than a century, people in the Kimberley encountered invading pastoralists, police, vigilantes, missionaries and, eventually, settlers, mining companies and the furthest-reaching tentacles of the global economy. They continued to practise ceremonies that celebrated the wirnan, and its laws became a rough blueprint for their own economic engagement with the increasing numbers of strangers and life-altering projects.

The flooding of a huge expanse of the lands of the Miriwoong and Gajirrabeng peoples in the East Kimberley to make Lake Argyle, the largest freshwater lake in Australia, was a shocking example of such a life-altering project in the late 1960s.

Miriwoong and Gajirrabeng peoples confronted the invaders when they arrived between 1885 and 1894 and set up cattle stations on areas now known as Newry, Argyle Downs, Lissadell, Ivanhoe and Carlton Hill.[18] The first town in this area was the port of Wyndham, which from 1886 provided sea access for ships to transport cattle. At the same time, there was a gold rush to the west and an influx of miners to Halls Creek, near the borders of the Gija and Jaru homelands. Indigenous people were massacred or removed from their lands, usually in chains, but survivors stayed on their country working, often in conditions of slavery, as 'station hands' for the White people. Then, with the construction of Kununurra and the Ord River Dam, and the flooding of a large part of the Ord River basin to create an irrigated agricultural region, Miriwoong and

Gajirrabeng people lost much of their lands to the new Diversion Dam and Lake Argyle.[19] The Mirima Reserve was gazetted in 1963 to confine them to an area on the edge of town, but with the introduction of equal wages and citizens' rights between 1961 and 1971, many moved into other parts of the new town, while others set up small communities on their traditional homelands, or *dawang*, in the region.[20] Through all of this, along with their neighbours, who included the Gija and others to the west, they maintained their wirnan ceremonies, affirming the cycle of exchange of powerful religious objects and maintaining the ancient reciprocal relationships and binding ties among the many groups who participated in several types of ceremony, including *joonba*.

Ceremonies of the joonba style, like Gurrir Gurrir and Binjyjirrminy, inspired the famous art movement of the East Kimberley. The work of the late artist Rover Thomas Joolama was in many ways inspired by Gurrir Gurrir and the homelands into which he was adopted. The wirnan is also conceived of as an economic relationship, legitimised by its spiritual basis, and its principles are used in everyday life as an economic logic.[21] Although Thomas was from the Canning Stock Route, much further to the south in Kukatja country,[22] he spent his last thirty years living in the East Kimberley at Warmun in Gija country.[23] In the mid-1970s, he found, or was given, the public Gurrir Gurrir ceremony through a deceased aunty in a dream, which eventually stimulated the production of art in the East Kimberley for broader audiences. To complement specific verses of the song series, pieces of plywood were painted with ochre and carried by dancers. Thomas and his uncle through ceremony, Paddy

Jaminji, painted many of these works on boards.[24] As artist Graham Cornall explains:

> The *Gurrir Gurrir* ceremony took the form of a 'palga', a narrative dance cycle, a vehicle by which both current and historical events and traditional spirit stories can be revealed in public … dancers carried, for each of the song-lines, painted boards or other constructions, most commonly crosses or similar simple geometric emblems made of light wooden frames and detailed with coloured woollen threads, and occasionally feathers and other materials, known as thread-crosses. The boards, which eventually escaped their ritual origins to become canvases created solely and intentionally as artworks, were originally little more than scraps of cardboard, or salvaged Masonite or three-ply off-cuts. As specific illustrations, the earliest Turkey Creek *Gurrir Gurrir* boards were usually relatively simple images illustrating a single site, spirit or event, raised on dark red ochre or black monochromatic grounds and rarely employing more than three 'colours'.[25]

THE SHOCK OF THE NEW

In the Kimberley in the 1980s, it was important for all visitors to take gifts, such as cartons of cigarettes, cowboy shirts with clip buttons, or hunting knives, and place them on a large canvas. The hosts would share the gifts among themselves. Later, as the cost of living became an issue, gifts were also expected to be cash. People needed to buy fuel for their vehicles. And whereas once the ceremonial food was a bullock, the catch from hunting, and damper made in the coals of the campfires, the advent of supermarkets and processed food placed pressure on ceremonial hosts to buy commercially produced foodstuffs. These gifts are simple acknowledgements of the wirnan, the hard work and generosity of ceremonial hosts, and the debt guests owe to them for allowing them to imbibe the power of their ritual.

The ceremonies, once held on Indigenous reserves and remote areas of cattle stations, have changed somewhat over the past four decades and their organisation has been supported by regional Indigenous ownership groups so that more people can attend. In the 1980s and 1990s, Indigenous ownership groups were formed to obtain land rights and protect civil rights and culture. With the recognition of native title and civil rights, ceremonies are now convened as parallel events with the annual general meetings of the Kimberley Land Council and the Kimberley Aboriginal Law and Culture Centre. The 1998 Stompem Ground Festival made Indigenous cultural expressions available to all comers, young and old, with rock bands, singers and dancers who had found new ways to live their culture – but the 'Culture Day' of the festival was reserved for visiting ceremonial dancers and singers.[26] Other parallel ceremonial events such as this are attached to formal *Kadiya* (Whitefella) meetings and festivals.

In the late 1990s, a joonba was found or dreamt by an elder born as Nyunkuny – better known among his peers as Goowoomji and by his English name, Paddy Bedford, or simply PB – when his career as an artist was about to soar with exhibitions and commissions at major art institutions. Goowoomji was born at Bedford Downs about four years after the Armistice was declared at the end of World War I. There was no armistice in Australia, however, where the frontier war waged by vigilantes, police and settlers against the Indigenous people in the Kimberley was the nation's dark secret. Two years before Goowoomji was born, the late Gamarliny (Timmy Timms) had also been born at Bedford Downs. He too became an artist in his later years. He and Goowoomji and others worked together to express their law in magnificent paintings, but also in ceremonial performances whose songs informed their works.

A couple of years before Goowoomji's birth, a group of his Gija relations had been murdered by strychnine poisoning in retaliation for the killing of one milking cow near Mount King, an Emu dreaming place to the west of the homestead. The massacre was organised by the then manager of Bedford Downs, Paddy Quilty. Indigenous people moved out to the government station at Violet Valley after this event, but by the time of the artist's birth they had been persuaded to return to work at Bedford Downs.

When Goowoomji was born, Quilty asked, 'Is it a boy or girl?'

'Oh, it's a boy,' was the reply.

Quilty said, 'You can call him Paddy after me.'

Goowoomji thus carried the name of a murderer, and he did so with deliberation to remind everyone of the massacre of his people. Eighty years later, he was able to tell the stories from that frontier to a wider audience. His astonishing artistic output, which began in his later years, refers often to his life on the cattle stations and the

Gija landscapes scarred by the cruelty of men such as Quilty and many others. His 2001 painting *Emu Dreaming and Bedford Downs Massacre*, and the 2002 work *Two Women Looking at the Bedford Downs Massacre Burning Place*, memorialise the ancestral spirits in those places and their tragic fates.

Goowoomji was a founding member of the Jirrawun Arts collective in the East Kimberley, and he dreamt one night the songs from *ngarranggarni* (ancestors) that concerned a massacre at Bedford Downs. The bodies of the murdered people, most of them Gija, were piled up by the White men who had poisoned them, and burnt in large pyres. He and his fellow law men and women transformed this dreamt joonba ceremony into a production entitled *Fire Fire Burning Bright*, staged by the Neminuwarlin Performance Group. Through their astounding performance of this theatre piece, incorporating a joonba song-and-dance ritual, history and innovative stagecraft, Neminuwarlin kept the law alive and remembered their ancestors.[27]

These narratives have become integrated with ngarranggarni and their ritual performances. The religious accounts connect mundane events to the spiritual world, as happened in Neminuwarlin's version. In the afterlife, dead men's spirits journey to historical places, through the ranges to the coast at Kunmunya, the location of the first Christian mission in the Kimberley, long since abandoned:

> After they die and their bodies are burnt, the spirits of the dead climb up the mountain to the west. They walk along the side of a cliff and look back to the fire where they had died, but

> eventually continue on travelling west until they meet a 'clever man' [ceremonial leader] and give him the song for the *joonba*. He tells the spirits that this is not their place and to go back to Kija country … then on to the distant seashore where they see a settlement with soldiers marching in lines. Being hungry in death as well as life, the spirits go to get fish from a man bringing them from the sea … 'the white man does not realise that these people are really spirits'.[28]

As well as the massacre sites now memorialised in sacred narratives, such as the one painted by Goowoomji, a sacred women's site where the Barramundi woman resides is one of many celebrated by women in the region. In one of her many efforts to protect workers at the Argyle diamond mine who strode over this dangerous women's site, the late Naangari (1930–2022), also known as Dirrmingali, Barratjil and Peggy Patrick,[29] painted a work called *Daiwul Ngarranggarni* (Barramundi Dreaming), depicting part of the story:

> … [A] female Barramundi … was being chased by a group of women from a waterhole near Kununurra all the way along the Blatchford Escarpment. As the Barramundi was being chased, she made frantic leaps to avoid her captors. These leaps carved gaps in the intervening ranges along the route and other marks showing her travels. The Barramundi went to a place known as Devil Devil Spring (located at the back of the Argyle Diamond Mine pit) which is where [Naangari's] painting of this story begins. The

> Barramundi twisted around and left marks in the rocks there. At Devil Devil Spring the women were trying to entrap her by using a traditional fishing method known as '*galgay*' in which rolls of Spinifex are used as a net to trap fish. The Barramundi leapt through the net and escaped. Where she leapt through the net, she left her white scales on a rock. Her huge leap carried her some distance where she landed and still lies. She turned into a rock and is seen now as Mt Pitt in the Pitt Range (known locally as Gundarriny).[30]

So it is with each life and journey to death, evading the traps so life can be reproduced, just as the Barramundi leaps along the river and through the net to breed. In Gija culture, the tension in such stories – whether from the ngarranggarni, the frontier, or both – is always partly resolved by an ending and left partly unresolved by cyclical repetition, as portrayed in ritual performances. This is expressed by various elements and by stories told and retold in the joonba, and in rituals such as the *manthe*, or 'welcome to country', involving the singing and smoking of guests by the traditional owners and guardians of sites.

These ceremonies gave the elders in the region the power to renegotiate the terms of the mining at Argyle. The people from the mining company, they asserted, had obligations under the wirnan law because they had damaged sites. One of these sacred places is a site cared for and celebrated solely by senior women associated with the sacred Barramundi woman, which had become the mine pit.

Another site was of primary significance to a group of senior men, including the late elder John Toby, and one of the most restricted sites under Indigenous law.

This is how the land speaks. There is a landscape behind the landscape, a powerful spiritual world, remembered in the ngarranggarni and continually performed in exciting and beautiful ceremonies to keep the law alive among the living.

A PRECIOUS INHERITANCE

Law is a precious inheritance. Its systems of descent and bequest are complex and fascinating. There is so much more to know about how people become holders of law as law men and law women. So far, we have looked at some attributes of law in the Yolŋu societies of north-east Arnhem Land and the Kimberley region, but several major regional systems of law are yet to be discussed. In western Arnhem Land, different approaches and subtleties can be mentioned. In desert regions, remarkable and world-renowned attributes of law became famous with the spread of anthropological knowledge about spiritual conception and what the travel writer Bruce Chatwin referred to as 'the songlines'.[31] There are distinctive regional legal systems in eastern Australia, with unique examples in eastern and western parts of Cape York Peninsula, north-western Queensland, much of New South Wales, and Victoria.

In the Torres Strait, which has two distinct east and west regions, there is the Law of Malo, which underpinned evidence in the *Mabo v Queensland (No 2)* native title case.[32] The chief justice of the High Court, Gerard Brennan, found that although Australia had been settled under the doctrine of terra nullius, it had not been 'uninhabited', and the notion that Indigenous peoples in Australia were 'barbarous' and 'without a settled law' was rejected.[33]

Today, however, Indigenous systems of law in Australia are vulnerable. They are at risk of being overwhelmed entirely by Crown law – especially the criminal justice system – and competing economic priorities. Yet it is important to remember that these systems of law were developed over many millennia and are tied inextricably to the original ancestors who shaped Australia and birthed its Indigenous people. This precious legacy deserves to survive, because its life-giving and life-affirming gifts can teach us all about how to live in Australia and the rest of the world and adapt to the critical challenges of our age.

3

EVERYTHING IS RELATED

Out of the land, our sounds become our words, our words become our stories, our stories become our songs, our songs become our ceremonies, our ceremonies become our teachings, our teachings become our beliefs, our beliefs become our law, and through that, we are strong and know who we are, wherever and whatever we are doing.

Wanta Pawu[1]

On Capital Hill in Canberra stands Australia's Parliament House. It was opened by Queen Elizabeth II on 9 May 1988 amid a year of public celebrations that marked the Australian Bicentenary – the 200th anniversary of the First Fleet's landing at Sydney Cove and founding of the colony of New South Wales on 26 January 1788. This date is still marked throughout Australia, though not without controversy, as Australia Day.

The ceremonious opening of Parliament House in 1988 was a main attraction of the official Australian Bicentenary program. The building's construction had cost $1.1 billion, involved 10,000 workers, and used 300,000 cubic metres of concrete and 24,000 tonnes of steel over a site of 32 hectares. Its facade was designed to align with the old Parliament House building, opened in 1927, along an axis facing Mount Ainslie over the waters of Lake Burley Griffin, and its intended functions were built along this axis into the building's geography: its easterly side houses the House of Representatives and its westerly side the Senate, its northerly entrance and central zone accommodate ceremonial and public spaces, and its southerly end lodges the executive government wing.

Parliament House is visited by some 760,000 people each year and around 5000 people work in the building when parliament sits. Among the many treasures to be seen there are selected works from the Parliament House art collection, which comprises more than 6000 items, including many significant pieces by Indigenous artists. One specific Indigenous work, however, was created as a permanent feature of the building's architecture. It is a sacred ancestral design that welcomes and farewells everyone who passes through its front entrance. Located in the Parliament House forecourt, under the crisp, clean air of Canberra's sky, is an oval-shaped ceremonial pool of water. Inside that pool, accessible by footbridges, is a circular island that represents the continent of Australia, and on that island is a mosaic spanning 196 square metres made from more than 90,000 individual hand-guillotined pieces of granite.

The mosaic's design is a licensed reproduction of a 1985 painting by the late, great Warlpiri artist Michael Jakamara Nelson. Born at Pikilyi in the Northern Territory, he lived at Yuendumu, where he was taken by his parents to attend school. The painting (reproduced in colour on the inside front cover of this book) is called *Possum and Wallaby Dreaming* and is based on a traditional Warlpiri sand painting used in public ceremonies. The six colours seen in the mosaic, and the painting on which it is based, were not randomly selected by Nelson. They were chosen to approximate the distinctive hues of the coloured sands that Warlpiri people of the Tanami Desert use in their elaborate sand-painting tradition. This involves gently pouring sand of different colours on to a clean-swept ground to create a ceremonial performance space filled with brilliant, dazzling imagery. The six colours used in *Possum and Wallaby Dreaming* are a light pinkish-red, yellow, green, blue, a deep earthy red, and white.

Around the centre of the design are the white-hot flames of a great fire, burning the deep red of the earth's surface. Out from there radiate the four other colours – light red, yellow, green and blue – which scorch the deep-red earth with their embers in a jigsaw patchwork of vibrant colours. Travelling across these colours into the centre of the design are the tracks of twelve animals – the possums and wallabies of the original painting's title. Three possums travel from the bottom right corner and another three from the top left corner, while three wallabies travel from the top right corner and another three from the bottom left corner. The shapes of their tracks show that all twelve animals are walking slowly on all fours in peace and humility towards the great fire at the centre.

This imagery of meeting and coming together from all corners of the land resonated strongly with the building's architects, who saw it as especially fitting for Parliament House's role as a meeting place for elected officials from throughout Australia.[2] This was certainly Nelson's intent when he created the painting. Having visited the site on Capital Hill before construction, he saw an important opportunity for his forecourt design to represent how systems of governance and law have long worked in Warlpiri society, in ways that both pre-date and continue to parallel the democratic processes in Parliament House. His design represents one of many Indigenous governance structures that existed in Australia long before the arrival of the First Fleet in 1788 yet are still largely unrecognised by the Commonwealth of Australia. It offers important insights into how good governance and decision-making can be understood from a Warlpiri perspective. Surrounded by the waters of its ceremonial pool, it is a mirror that reflects the workings of Parliament House from an Indigenous perspective grounded in millennia of ancestral law.

HOME WITHIN

Possum and Wallaby Dreaming is a depiction of a Warlpiri *Jardiwarnpa* ceremony as written in the ancestral language of sand painting. In Warlpiri tradition, the Jardiwarnpa is an entirely public annual purification ceremony in which children and adults of all ages and sexes can participate. Importantly, it is the first in a cycle of ceremonies that Warlpiri people traditionally perform each year, and its purpose is to maintain peace and order in Warlpiri society by laying to rest all disagreements, enmities and hostilities of the year gone by. It usually starts in October, upon the breaking of the wet season, when the earth is so hot underfoot it can burn the soles of your feet, and it uses the searing heat of fire to burn giant sheaves of grass as a means of purifying all participants.

Because this ceremony's function is to lay enmities to rest, the term Jardiwarnpa can be translated into English as 'deep sleep'. Only once this process is completed can ensuing ceremonies in the annual cycle take place, which involve the training of future leaders and the meeting of senior elders to negotiate agreements and make decisions. The Jardiwarnpa ceremony therefore brings people together from all corners of the Warlpiri homelands in the Tanami Desert to start the annual process of enacting ancestral law. As indicated by the slow pace of the animal tracks towards the great fire depicted at the centre of *Possum and Wallaby Dreaming*, all participants must enter the Jardiwarnpa ceremony with a humble attitude before the law and with the peaceful intent of laying past animosities to rest.

The five concentric rings of white dots that depict the great fire at the centre of *Possum and Wallaby Dreaming* indicate that the Jardiwarnpa ceremony is typically a large gathering that brings together different groups from across Warlpiri society. Overall, Warlpiri society consists of four main groups who hold responsibility for producing different parts of four main ceremonies performed in each annual cycle. The groups are called *Wanya-parnta* (Emu), *Parra* (Day), *Wawirri* (Red Kangaroo) and *Munga* (Night), and each is associated with a colour: Emu is blue, depicting water; Day is green, depicting vegetation; Red Kangaroo is red, depicting blood; and Night is yellow, depicting stars. These four colours are shown in the blue, green, light-red and yellow clusters of dots that radiate out from the great fire in *Possum and Wallaby Dreaming*, representing the many different Warlpiri homelands across the Tanami Desert.

The patchwork pattern indicates how the four main Warlpiri groups own these different homelands.

The way these groups are related in Warlpiri law binds together everyone in society. While group membership always passes from father to child within a family, the system ensures that everyone in Warlpiri society is descended from someone in each of the four main groups. The artist Michael Jakamara Nelson, for example, who is in the Red Kangaroo group, would have one grandparent in each of the four groups. His *warringi* (father's father) would also be in the Red Kangaroo group, but his *jinngardi* (father's mother) would be in the Day group, his *jaja* (mother's mother) in the Emu group, and his *jamirdi* (mother's father) in the Night group.

The name Warlpiri is a contraction of *warlpa-wiri* (big winds), in reference to the high winds that characteristically sweep across the Tanami Desert. Each of the four main Warlpiri groups is therefore also associated with a cardinal wind direction: the Emu group is *Yatitjarra* (North), the Day group is *Kakarrara* (East), the Red Kangaroo group is *Kurlirra* (South) and the Night group is *Karlarra* (West). In *Possum and Wallaby Dreaming*, these are the four cardinal directions from which the four groups of animals travel, representing the journeys of the four main Warlpiri groups to ceremony.

Pulyaranyi by Wanta Pawu (see Figure 2), also shows each of the four main groups travelling to meet for a Jardiwarnpa ceremony along their respective *pulyaranyi* (windblown path) from the four cardinal directions.[3] Each group's homeland on this design's periphery, depicted by the four concentric circles, is protected from the high desert winds by a large, thick, arched windbreak.

FIGURE 2: Wanta Pawu, *Pulyaranyi*, 2012

The windblown path travelled by each group is represented by the six parallel lines connecting each homeland to the Jardiwarnpa at the centre. The great ceremony, where all four groups meet, is again shown by the five concentric circles at the centre of Wanta's design.

These directional alignments are further complemented by links to the seasonal cycle of the Tanami Desert. The Emu group is associated with the annual wet season, the Day group with the following cool season, the Red Kangaroo with the dry season, and the Night group with the hot season.

In its totality, this detailed system of connecting people with their homelands, the seasons and the environment is a way of enabling people to locate themselves within their families as well as within space and time. This is fundamental to Wanta's compelling philosophy of ngurra-kurlu (home-having), which he has developed through his public education work as a way to understand how to live in Australia as one's home, and carry that sense of home within. This, Wanta says, is the birthright of all people born in Australia.[4] For Warlpiri people, he identifies five fundamental principles for maintaining ngurra-kurlu within oneself: jaru (language), warlalja (kin), kuruwarru (law), manyuwana (ceremony) and walya (land). Without understanding these five principles, he says, people lose themselves and their purpose, and become homeless in their own land.[5]

One final significant feature of the Warlpiri social system, for now, is that all four main groups are equal and responsible to each other under law. All four groups have senior elders who are qualified and authorised through the formal learning processes of the annual ceremonial cycle to negotiate agreements and make decisions on behalf of their groups, but these agreements and decisions must also be confirmed by the other three groups, whose views carry equal weight. Because all four groups are closely related through family structures, each has a vested interest in delivering good outcomes for all. That each group also holds responsibility for each producing different parts of four main annual ceremonies serves to assure their cooperation even further. Overall, this system,[6] as founded by the original ancestors, is designed to ensure that no one group or family lineage can dominate the whole of society, and that the needs of all are continually negotiated and balanced to provide the best possible social outcomes. This is the principal way that balance of power is maintained among different groups in Warlpiri society.

FINDING BALANCE

Maintaining the balance of power through marriage and descent law can be considered a primary goal of the ways that Indigenous societies across Australia are organised. As Indigenous societies have often had relatively small populations, maintaining systems that regulate who can marry whom also ensures that marriages are not too close and that there is an even spread of marriageable partners across the whole of society. Consequently, who can inherit the many different homelands held by different groups within a society is also evenly spread. Even in major cities today, intimate knowledge of kinship and bloodlines is held within families and relayed as required to ensure that marriages are contracted in such a way as to avoid marriages between people who are too closely related, particularly given the tumultuous histories that have disrupted so many communities.

Indigenous concepts and practices involving family and inheritance are very different from those used in the English language, and have no direct translations. Anthropologists have therefore established some rather unwieldy terms to describe the different ways that Indigenous societies in Australia are organised. Basically, the terms *moiety*, *semimoiety*, *section* and *subsection* are used to describe broad groupings within Indigenous societies that govern property rights and marriage rules.[7] The four main groups in Warlpiri society, for example, are classified by anthropologists as *patri-semimoieties* – with the prefix *patri-* indicating that group membership is inherited through male lines – even though Warlpiri people themselves might simply prefer to call each one a *turnu* or group. None of these grouping types is found in universal usage across Australia. However, they are often at least partially combined in different regions in distinctive ways.

The term 'moiety' describes any society that is divided into two main groups. In Australia, there are *generational moieties*, *patrimoieties* and *matrimoieties*. A *generational moiety* system separates parents and children into two alternating moieties. Your own moiety includes your brothers, sisters and cousins, as well as your grandparents two generations up and your grandchildren two generations down. The other moiety includes your fathers, mothers, uncles and aunts one generation up, and your children, nephews and nieces one generation down. You marry someone in your own moiety but are descended from people over generations in both moieties. The Ngaatjatjarra people of the Western Desert, for example, have two generational moieties called *Tjintultukultul* (Sun-side) and *Ngumpaluru* (Shade-side). They also use relative terms to describe 'our moiety' and 'your moiety' – *Nganatarka* (We bone) and *Tjanamilytjan* (They flesh) – evoking a greater societal body comprising two essential parts.

In a *patrimoiety* system, you belong to the same moiety as your father and marry someone of the opposite moiety. Everyone is descended from people in both moieties, irrespective of the moiety alignment you inherit through your male lineage. Yolŋu society in north-east Arnhem Land has two patrimoieties, *Dhuwa* and *Yirritja*. Yolŋu people consider these to be the two named constitutions of Yolŋu law, as created by different sets of founding ancestors. The anthropological term moiety, from *medius* (middle) in Latin, implies that Dhuwa and Yirritja are two halves of a greater social whole. But it is important to note that, in Yolŋu law, each of these constitutions is whole unto itself. There are some sixty Yolŋu clans who own many different homelands across north-east Arnhem Land. Like patrimoiety membership, clan membership is inherited from father to child. Roughly half of all Yolŋu clans are Dhuwa and the others are Yirritja. The whole of Yolŋu society therefore rests on the cooperation of Dhuwa and Yirritja clans through their intermarriage in each generation. All Yolŋu children have both a Dhuwa parent and a Yirritja parent, thereby ensuring this balance. As a Yolŋu child, you inherit your clan's homelands and ceremonies though your male lineage, but hold various other rights in the homelands and ceremonies of other clans to whom you are related through your female lineage.[8]

In a *matrimoiety* system, you belong to the same moiety as your mother and marry someone of the opposite moiety, with descent rights, of course, flowing to people through both lineages. The Ngiyampaa language of central-north New South Wales names two matrimoieties, *Ngarawan* and *Muwambuwan*. In this system, all children have both a Ngarawan parent and a Muwambuwan parent, but trace primary descent and matrimoiety membership through their female lineages.[9]

A semimoiety system adds an additional layer of separation in determining suitable marriage partners. Among the Marra people of north-west Queensland, for example, there are four patri-semimoieties called *Murrungun*, *Mambali*, *Burdal* and *Guyal*. Murrungun and Mambali are both in the *Muluri* patrimoiety, while Burdal and Guyal are in the *Umbana* patrimoiety. Like patrimoiety membership, membership of each patri-semimoiety is inherited from father to child through the male lineage. Everyone in this system still marries someone of the opposite patrimoiety. The addition of patri-semimoieties here, however, ensures that your marriage partner is not from the same patri-semimoiety as your own mother. A Burdal person whose mother is Murrungun can thus only marry a person who is Mambali. But a Burdal person cannot marry a Guyal person, because they are in the same patri-semimoiety.[10]

A section system emerges when generational moieties, patrimoieties and matrimoieties are all recognised and superimposed simultaneously. They sort all people in society into four equal groups or sections. The four sections do not have proper names of their own but instead provide a full set of eight names, comprising a female name and a male name in each section, that can be used by people as personal names in addition to their given names. In Aboriginal English, these kinds of names are commonly called 'skin names'. This concept of the skin name, however, usually comes from the word for 'meat' or 'flesh' in Indigenous languages. Your skin name is a generic moniker that someone may call out as a term of endearment or use to protect your identity under uncertain or perilous circumstances.

Your skin name locates you on an interpersonal grid that scopes all possible relationships in society, which are always expressed via a finite set of kin terms, no matter how closely or distantly you might be related to other individuals. Skin names and associated kin terms also tend to recur in families once they start describing relatives three generations away from your own. The kin term you would call your *father's father's father's father*, for example, is *brother*. That makes his son – that is, your *father's father's father* – your son also. Once you know someone else's skin name, even if that person is a total stranger, you will know what kin term to call them and how you should behave around them.

If a total stranger who becomes an acquaintance does not have a recognisable skin name in their own language, then you would normally give them an appropriate one from your own language, depending largely on your own perceived seniority to them. For example, colleagues at similar levels in a workplace might decide that they will relate as *sisters*, while a student might call his teacher *father*. This practice of inviting new acquaintances to relate to you by using your own kin terms is widespread across Australia and is commonly called *adoption* in Aboriginal English. Though often misinterpreted as an inability on the part of Indigenous Australians to relate to newcomers in any other way, this kind of adoption practice ensures that all engagements with newcomers are conducted respectfully and in keeping with ancestral law. This is mainly because, ultimately, no one can be above the law.[11]

As regional kinship systems are often observed across vast distances, marriage and descent relationships between skin names sometimes vary in different localities. In the Ngiyampaa language of central-north New South Wales, each section has a pair of male and female skin names that always sit in a brother-and-sister relationship. In one realisation of this framework, these are the *Kampu* and *Putha* brother-sister pairing of the Muwambuwan matrimoiety, who marry the *Marr* and *Matha* brother-sister pairing of the Ngarawan matrimoiety. Similarly, the *Yipay* and *Yipatha* brother-sister pairing of the Muwambuwan matrimoiety marry the *Kapi* and *Kapitha* brother-sister pairing of the Ngarawan matrimoiety.[12] If a Kapi meets another Kapi, even if that person is a total stranger, then they are brothers and can engage with each other as brothers. If a Kapi meets a Matha, he shows her the same care he shows his own mother. A Kapi would only ever seek to marry a Yipatha and would treat her mother, a Putha, with extraordinary deference to the extent that he would do her bidding but only address her through other people. This last kind of in-law relationship is what, in English and Aboriginal English respectively, is called an 'avoidance' or 'poison' relationship. More accurately, it is an expression of deep respect, particularly of sons-in-law for their mothers-in-law.

Identifying and exercising functional social relationships between individuals is always possible so long as they follow the logic of such kinship laws. When younger men first marry, for example, they often partner with older women. Similarly, when women are young, they usually marry older men. Much older men of proven good character can be married to more than one wife at a time and, in regions where skin names are used, each of their wives will have a compatible skin name. Anthropologists call this practice polygynous marriage, from *polygyne* (many women) in Greek. When a woman's husband passes away, it often falls to one of his surviving brothers to continue caring for her as a wife, in what anthropologists call a levirate marriage, from *levir* (husband's brother) in Latin. These arrangements persist in some remote parts of Australia today. However, because they were often banned by missionaries and assimilationist governments, it is now common for people of the same generation to marry. Nonetheless, even in cases where a region's original kinship terminology has been largely replaced by English terms, local Indigenous kinship and marriage rules will usually still be observed.

The complex flow of relationships between wives and husbands, parents and children, around the matrix of skin names within section systems works to ensure the even distribution of interests and resources throughout society. Whereas section systems typically have four sections containing eight skin names, four female and four male, 'subsection' systems add an additional layer of separation in determining suitable marriage partners. They have eight sections containing sixteen skin names, eight female and eight male. Superimposed over its four patri-semimoieties, Warlpiri society uses a subsection system containing sixteen skin names. Each of the four patri-semimoieties contains four skin names, two male and two female, which express alternating father-to-child relationships through the male lineage. There is no strong sense of clan at a distributed level in Warlpiri society. Generally, the many different Warlpiri homelands and their associated ceremonies are evenly distributed across the four patri-semimoieties, and individuals are primarily inheritors of homelands through their fathers' lineages. Because the Tanami Desert is so vast, spanning 184,500 square kilometres in size, the composition of the four main annual Warlpiri ceremonies varies across different families. The precise sequence discussed throughout this book is thus the one most closely observed by Wanta's family. This means that Warlpiri people put extraordinary effort into ensuring that babies are born on homelands that properly align with their respective patri-semimoieties and responsibilities to country through their male lineages.

PULYARANYI

As discussed above, the Warlpiri kinship system is quite exceptional in simultaneously recognising two generational moieties, two matrimoieties, two patrimoieties, four patri-semimoieties, eight subsections and sixteen gendered skin names. These perfectly mirrored and balanced parameters ensure the even distribution of

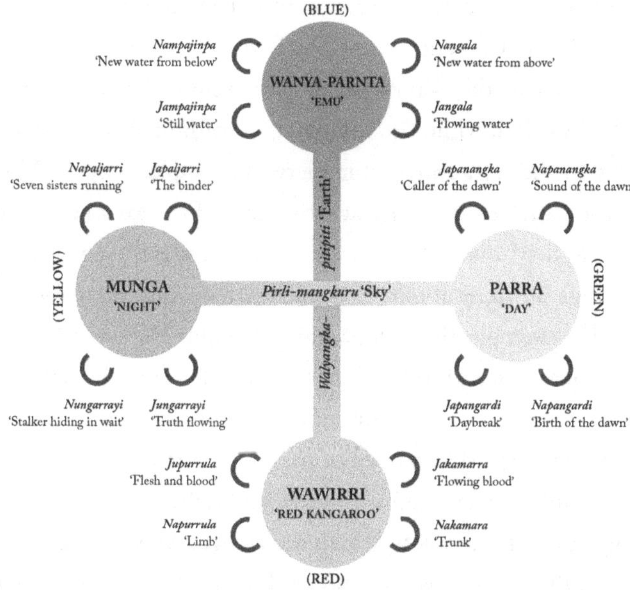

FIGURE 3: Warlpiri skin names, their meanings, and the axial relationships between pairs of patri-semimoities that form the two patrimoities, *Walyangka-pitipiti* (Earth) and *Pirli-mangkuru* (Sky).

legal authority and resources across the whole of Warlpiri society. Figures 3 and 4, based on Wanta Pawu's *Pulyaranyi* (see Figure 2), show the complex interrelationships within Warlpiri society.[13]

Figure 3 shows the four patri-semimoities (Wanya-parnta, Parra, Wawirri and Munga), the four skin names contained within each, as indicated by the surrounding semicircles, representing sitting people, and the meaning of the skin names. The vertical and horizontal axes that connect the patri-semimoieties form two patrimoieties, called *Walyangka-pitipiti* (Earth), comprising Wanya-parnta and Wawirri, and *Pirli-mangkuru* (Sky), comprising Parra and Munga. It is along these two axes that cooperation in producing four main ceremonies within the annual cycle occurs. The Jardiwarnpa ceremony is started for everyone by the Wanya-parnta patri-semimoiety and completed by the Wawirri, while the following *Kurdiji* (Shield) ceremony is started by the Parra patri-semimoiety and completed by the Munga.

The patri-semimoieties at either end of the axes, such as Parra (Day) and Munga (Night), are said to reflect each other. The meanings of the skin names in each patri-semimoiety follow this logic. For example, the skin names in the blue Wanya-parnta patri-semimoiety all have meanings associated with water and reflect those in the red Wawirri patri-semimoiety, which are all associated with blood. Similarly, skin names of the green Parra patri-semimoiety have meanings associated with birth and reflect those in the yellow Munga patri-semimoiety, which are associated with death. In this context, the Sun births each day on Earth, while the constellations in the night sky are the campfires of the old people and the eternal home to which all souls eventually return.

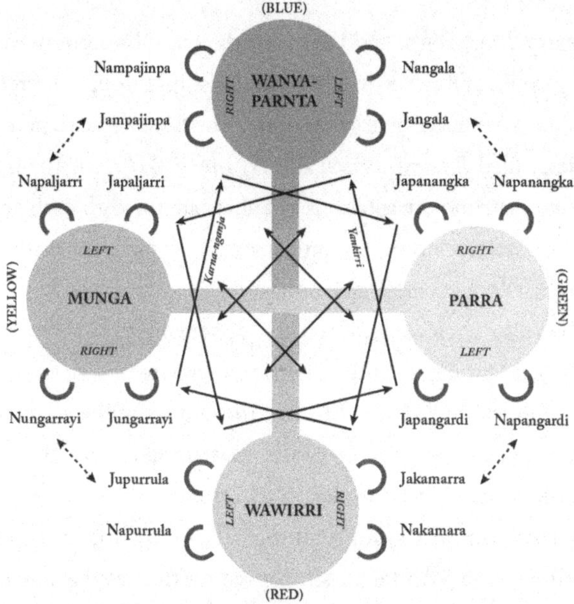

FIGURE 4: Matrimoiety affiliations via mother-to-child descent (–>), and ideal (<—>) and alternative (< - - - >) marriage choices among patri-semimoieties (O) and skin names (∩) in Warlpiri society.

Figure 4 describes in more detail the structures that guide relations between skin names and patri-semimoieties. The four skin names in each patri-semimoiety are sorted by both gender and matrimoiety. Skin names that begin with the letter J are male, while those beginning with the letter N are female. The matrimoiety alignment of each skin name is indicated by the 'Right' and 'Left' labels in each patri-semimoiety. In the Warlpiri language, the proper names of these two matrimoieties are *Karnanganja* (I am going to eat and drink), which is 'Right', and *Yankirri* (people coming and going), which is 'Left'. Like the two patrimoieties, these two matrimoieties must also intermarry. These Right and Left matrimoieties also form two counter-rotating cycles of mother-to-child relationships through discrete sets of skin names over successive generations. There are also two generational moieties, called *Janamiljarnpa* and *Nganarntarrka*, which also follow these two matrimoiety rotations but alternate through each successive patri-semimoiety and do not intermarry.[14] People must instead marry within their own generational moiety.

Overall, this simultaneous observance of generational moiety, matrimoiety and patrimoiety separations ensures that any marriageable partner for any individual will be of the same generational moiety, the opposite matrimoiety and the opposite patrimoiety, as required under Warlpiri law. The use of skin names makes this complex system simple. It is easy, for example, for a Jampijinpa, like Wanta, to simply know that he is marriageable to either a Napangardi or a Napaljarri without needing to think through the complex mechanisms we have outlined here.[15]

This social organisation system is likely one of the most sophisticated to be found anywhere on Earth, and its design is far from arbitrary. Like everything in Indigenous law, it is inspired by and built on a paradigm found in nature that serves as a constant reminder for how authority and resources should always be evenly distributed across the whole of society. This fundamental tenet of sharing and fair dealing remains important and relevant to Indigenous people today, no matter where in Australia their homelands are.

CRUX AUSTRALIS

Wheeling overhead in the sky every night, visible throughout Australia and the Southern Hemisphere year round, is the constellation Crux, commonly known as the Southern Cross. Lying at the southern end of the Milky Way's visible band, it holds an important place in Warlpiri law and in the legal systems of various other Indigenous groups in Australia. Warlpiri and other desert peoples commonly wear a single white feather as a headdress in ceremonies that represents the Southern Cross. In Warlpiri law, its four brightest outer stars provide a binding logic that maps the workings of all reality, as shown in Figure 5. Read clockwise from the bottom in order of diminishing brightness, its brightest star, Alpha (α) Crucis, is associated with the Wanya-parnta patri-semimoiety, while Beta (β) Crucis, Gamma (γ) Crucis and Delta (δ) Crucis are respectively associated with the Parra, Wawirri and Munga patri-semimoieties. All other Warlpiri associations of these four patri-semimoieties with colours, cardinal directions, seasons, homelands, ceremonies and skin names also map onto these four outer stars.

The Southern Cross is the basis of the four cardinal directions and four homeland colours seen in Michael Jakamara Nelson's painting *Possum and Wallaby Dreaming*. It is the basis of Wanta Pawu's *Pulyaranyi* design and ngurra-kurlu philosophy, and, ultimately, the basis of the Warlpiri social organisation system itself.[16] It is a paradigm found in nature upon which all Warlpiri law is based, which promotes understanding of how everything in reality is related to everything else. It reminds us that we humans, at

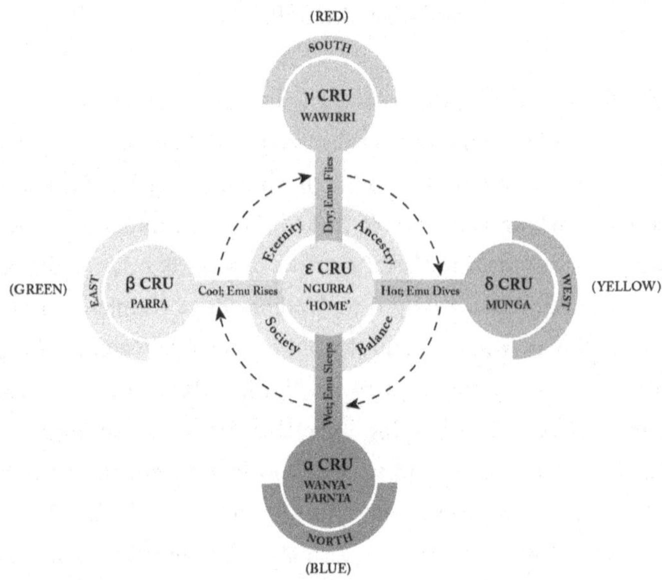

FIGURE 5: The Southern Cross as read in Warlpiri law. Its brightest star, Alpha Crucis, is positioned at the bottom and aligns with the Wanya-parnta patri-semimoiety's opening of the Jardiwarnpa ceremony. The three following ceremonies are aligned with ever-fainter stars as they ascend towards full leadership training. The central star, though the faintest, is the most important of all and represents balance among all things (see Chapter 7).

an atomic level, are made of the same stuff as all things in creation, including the stars in the Southern Cross itself.

The Southern Cross is seen to rotate through the sky all night, every night, gradually changing position in relation to Earth's horizon throughout each year. When the brightest star of the Southern Cross is positioned away from the horizon at the top, to its right are the two stars of the Pointers, which form a woman's ceremonial digging stick, and to its left are two Magellanic clouds, which form the entry and exit holes of a goanna's nest. These two adjacent constellations respectively represent the Right and Left matrimoieties, Karnanganja and Yankirri. In the hot season, usually in October, the time of the year to commence the annual cycle of ceremonies is marked by the digging-stick Pointers touching Earth's horizon. At this time, the Southern Cross is hidden behind the curvature of the Earth and forms a great *yarla* (yam) upon which all who gather for ceremonies will feast, emphasising that knowledge, like food, provides nourishment.[17]

In Warlpiri designs based on the Southern Cross, the faint fifth inner star, Epsilon (ε) Crucis, is always positioned perfectly in the centre, where the vertical and horizontal axes cross. It represents a perfect point of balance, when all things in creation are moving and working in harmony and when the old people and their living kin feel calm and satisfied at the state of the world. This utopian state of grace is, of course, unattainable, at least in the longer term. Accordingly, the inner star of the Southern Cross is not positioned perfectly in the centre. It is skewed so far off centre that it is nearly in line between Alpha Crucis and Delta Crucis. For the Warlpiri people, this serves as an indelible reminder that nothing in life can be taken for granted and that rule of law is not a given. Everything in law and life requires constant effort and work, from good governance and decision-making among leaders to maintaining harmony within your own family and peace within society. The Southern Cross is a permanent reminder that we must always strive through our observance of law to achieve and sustain this balance.

RISING OVER HOME

The Law of Malo of the Torres Strait, which informed the success of the *Mabo v Queensland (No 2)* case in overturning terra nullius in 1992 (see Chapter 1), is similarly linked to the stars.[18] In Meriam oral tradition, four brothers sailed south to the Torres Strait from New Guinea.[19] A strong wind caused them to separate and the canoe of one brother, Malo, sank at the island called Mer. Malo

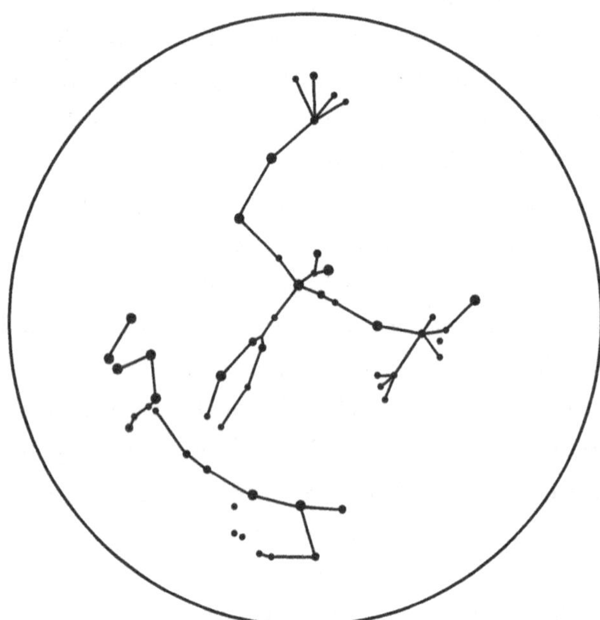

FIGURE 6: The large Tagai constellation, which incorporates parts (or all) of the Crux, Corvus, Centaurus, Lupus and Scorpius constellations. Tagai is an important creation ancestor for Torres Strait Islanders and his story and behaviour inform the traditional Torres Strait Islander way of life.

then named the land and its environmental features, established traditional law, and became the primary ancestral figure of Mer's people. One of Malo's laws is that because every star follows its own path, so will each person.[20]

For Torres Strait Islanders, the Sun, Moon and stars inform all law for navigation, calendars, weather prediction, seasons, food economics, ceremonies and social structure.[21] This knowledge underlies all Torres Strait Islander traditions, as recorded and handed down through traditional songs, dances and designs.[22] Astronomical knowledge also contains practical information about the natural world and guides how Torres Strait Islander people understand their environment.

Torres Strait Islander understandings of identity are also linked to Tagai, the creation ancestor who is represented by a constellation of stars spanning the night sky (see Figure 6). Tagai was a great warrior and fisherman.[23] He had a crew of twelve men called *Zugubals* and a confidant and deputy named Kareg. The group went reef fishing but did not catch any fish, so Tagai left to search for a more suitable spot. While he was gone, the Zugubals grew hungry, tired and frustrated in the heat. They ate all of their food and drank all of their water, including, foolishly, Tagai's food and water. When he returned, he was furious. He tied the men into two groups of six and cast them into the sea, where they drowned. They went into the sky and formed two constellations, the *Usiam* (Pleiades) and *Utimal* or *Seg* (Orion's belt and scabbard), while Tagai and Kareg went to the other side of the sky to keep away from them.

Tagai is a very large constellation. In his left hand he holds a spear, indicated by the Southern Cross, and in his right a native cherry fruit, represented by the constellation Corvus. His head and body, meanwhile, consist of stars in Centaurus and Lupus. He is standing on the bow of his canoe, which is traced by the body of Scorpius, and Kareg is the star Antares at the stern. Their appearance in the morning and evening throughout the year informs seasonal change, food economics and social structure.

Tagai provides law for four tenets that govern the Torres Strait Islander way of life. The first is that the stars of Tagai hold knowledge and spirituality for future generations; the second is that Torres Strait Islanders are a seafaring people; the third relates to the laws and order of the world as instructed by Tagai; and the fourth established the life cycle as a period of time and renewal based on the Sun, the Moon, and the rising and setting of certain stars.

Lunar phases link to changing tides, a relationship that is well understood by Torres Strait Islanders. Elders teach that the best time to fish is during a low neap tide during the first or last quarter Moon, rather than a higher spring tide during the new or full Moon phase. During a neap tide, the water is clearer and fish are calmer, making them easier to catch.

People plant their gardens by the phases of the Moon. The cusps or tips of *kerkar meb*, the crescent Moon, point in different directions throughout the year. When they point upwards (*meb metalug em*), the Moon looks like a bowl collecting water. This occurs during the fine weather of the dry *Sager* season, when the sea is choppy and cumulus clouds form in the sky. When the Moon tilts on its side (*meb uag em*), the water pours out of the bowl and falls as the rains of the wet *Kuki* season. The seas are calm, with a flat, mirrored surface, thin cirrus clouds form in the sky, and a fuzzy halo can sometimes form around the Moon. Moon halos created by cold low fronts can be used to forecast weather, and in the Torres Strait, the *susri* or ring around the Moon is seen as a hut built by the Moon-Man to shield himself from coming rain.[24]

As in other Indigenous traditions of Australia, all of this Torres Strait Islander law is recorded and handed down through extensive bodies of traditional songs, dances and designs. The dance song 'Gedge Togia', for example, accompanied by two long-waisted *warup* drums, sings of how the Moon rises over home. When Meriam elders litigated against the Australian Government over sea rights in 2005,[25] the opposition lawyer claimed that the Torres Strait Islands were all separate enclaves with little or no contact between them. Meriam elder Alo Tapim successfully argued against this assumption by singing 'Gedge Togia', which contains sections in separate languages from two different islands, thereby demonstrating the extensive contact between them.[26]

4

RESPECT AND RESPONSIBILITY

There is an important detail of the *Possum and Wallaby Dreaming* mosaic in the Parliament House forecourt that can be easy to miss if you are unable to read Australian animal tracks. It can be read in the postures shown by the tracks of the six possums and six wallabies as they approach the great fire at the design's centre. They do not race towards the central fire of the Jardiwarnpa ceremony with careless abandon. Rather, they gather for the ceremony slowly and peacefully, walking on all fours in humility and respect for themselves, each other and the law.

The intended message here is clear. Respect for oneself and for others – and indeed all things in creation – and humility before ancestors and their laws form the basic currency that has enabled

Indigenous societies in Australia to develop and thrive across the continent. Given by the original ancestors and observed over countless generations by those who have gone before, these systems encourage people to maintain the social good and strive towards balance in all things. They instil people with good values and encourage beneficial behaviours.

The need for people to approach life with underlying respect and humility, as ceremonies teach, is essential for the proper functioning of societies in keeping with ancestral law. The legal systems established by the original ancestors work to provide standards and protections that help societies function and maintain their standards of living. They actively encourage humble, thoughtful and peaceful behaviours in line with an underlying ethos of respect and work to discourage and dissipate behaviours that are needlessly selfish, aggressive and destructive.

RESPECT EVERYTHING

As discussed in Chapter 3, the Warlpiri Jardiwarnpa purification ceremony is open to participants of all ages and sexes. It works to affirm peace and order by laying to rest all disagreements, enmities and hostilities of the past year. By participating in it, people agree to terms of appropriate conduct in a way that is binding under Warlpiri law. Ensuing ceremonies in the annual cycle involve the training of future leaders and meetings of senior leaders to negotiate agreements and make decisions. Because these ensuing ceremonies can only take place once the Jardiwarnpa has been completed, the assent of all participants to the binding terms of this first annual ceremony is essential for Warlpiri society to function properly.

The Wiradjuri concept of *yindyamarra* (respect) from central New South Wales beautifully conveys this pivotal ideal. The 2015 short film *Yindyamarra Yambuwan* (Respect Everything), directed by Bernard Sullivan in collaboration with Flo Grant, Stan Grant Senior and other Wiradjuri elders, vividly shows how this concept of mutual respect has multiple intersecting meanings, including to 'give honour, go slow, take responsibility, and think before acting'.[1] Recently, with the consent of Wiradjuri elders, Charles Sturt University, which has campuses on Wiradjuri homelands, has adopted *yindyamarra winhanganha* as an expression of its core ethos. The phrase has been translated for this purpose as 'the wisdom of respectfully knowing how to live well in a world worth living in'.[2]

In the Yolŋu languages of north-east Arnhem Land, the term *raypirri'* conveys another facet of Indigenous ideas concerning respect. It can refer to a reprimand for doing the wrong thing. However, as identified by the Yolŋu Aboriginal Consultants Initiative at Charles Darwin University, it also reflects the concept of self-discipline in 'congruence with the proper ancestral way of doing things'.[3] This stems from common Indigenous understandings and processes of keeping and following law as a preferred way of living that honours people and their sacred bonds with ancestors, homelands and all things.

This kind of respect is ideally taught and maintained by people through all stages of their lives, from infancy to old age. It is observed and practised through everyday acts and routines in all kinds of ways, from caring for children and helping old people to sharing food and cleaning up at home. It is when you participate in ancestral ceremonies, however, that values and behaviours of respect and humility are taught and observed in their most formal settings.

Before the gradual expansion of schools and universities across the continent in the 20th century, Indigenous ceremonial processes and teachings had provided the only known systems of formal education in Australia for 65,000 years. Mirroring the travels and actions of the original ancestors as they founded homelands and made laws for people of their descent, ceremonial processes teach and contextualise the appropriate behaviours and values that people should aspire to emulate in their daily lives. They also model and demonstrate the catastrophic consequences of bad behaviours, such as those rooted in greed and jealousy, that should be avoided. People infer and transmit all kinds of useful interpretations of ancestral deeds as ways of identifying and setting expectations around beneficial and harmful behaviours.

At a more fundamental level, however, most of the original ancestors have no underlying moral motivations. Like the various species and other natural phenomena whose forms they take, there are no good or bad intentions behind their behaviours: they simply exist and act according to the natural logic of their own behavioural cycles. For example, Rainbow Serpent ancestors can form wet-season thunderstorms that yield destructive lightning and deadly floods, but the rains they bring can also nourish new life and growth where they fall.

Among the Gumatj, a Yolŋu clan of north-east Arnhem Land, the ancestor Bäru (Saltwater Crocodile) is revered both as a swift and cunning hunter and for the care it gives its newborn young when nesting. Indeed, all Yolŋu clans typically trace descent from various species that bring life and vitality but can also be *ma̲dakarritj* (ferocious) in their capacity to inflict pain or kill when hunting or protecting their nests. The various ways that these revered ancestral species hunt and defend themselves inform the very same practices among people in Yolŋu clans.

Nature makes no concessions for human needs and wants. Both thunderstorms and saltwater crocodiles can kill you if you have not been properly taught how to live and behave around them. Showing respect for all things in nature by being observant of their workings and learning about the potential benefits and dangers they present is therefore another important way that people follow law and the proper ancestral way of doing things. Wanta Pawu has explained how, in the Warlpiri language, the word *wala* describes feelings of trust, ease, happiness, gladness, satisfaction and pride that flow when law is properly observed and all things in creation are moving and working in harmony.[4]

In this way, following law is considered pivotal to maintaining holistic health and wellbeing, both physically and spiritually, across personal, social and environmental domains. Yolŋu people hold that following law, by diligently working to prepare and participate in ceremonies and by being respectful and helpful to others in everyday life, is a primary way to accumulate *märr*. This term has no direct equivalent in English, but it connotes a sense of the inner strength, enlightenment and wellbeing that can be derived from ancestral power. Märr might be envisioned as a muscle of the soul that can grow in strength when a person does the right thing by following law. It can be built up over time by being a generally good person and diligently following law, and it can dwindle if a bad lifepath is taken. Overall, people who accumulate greater märr are thought to be more stable, fruitful and fulfilled, better candidates for marriage and parenthood, and better suited to positions of authority and leadership.[5]

The attainment of strong märr is a key benefit that flows from following law and doing things in the proper ancestral way. This core virtue is commonly recognised in different languages across Australia – the equivalent term, for example, in the Yawuru language of the Kimberley region is *liyan*. As explained by Patrick Dodson, former Chair of the Yawuru Native Title Holders Aboriginal Corporation and now a senator for Western Australia:

> *Liyan* is about relationships, family, community and what gives meaning to people's lives … Connection to country and … our culture and society is fundamental to having good *liyan*. When we feel disrespected or abused our *liyan* is bad, which can be insidious and corrosive for both the individual and the community. When our *liyan* is good our wellbeing and everything else is in a good space.[6]

ROOT AND BRANCH

Yolŋu legal processes are built on the concept of rom. This, as we discussed in Chapter 2, corresponds to the concept of 'law' in English, yet also shares the extended meanings of culture, proper practice and the ancestral way.[7] Overall, rom is the common term for the body of ancestral laws handed down from the original ancestors over countless generations. It is informed by observations of the Yolŋu homelands that the original ancestors made to guide their living descendants in the right ways to do things. Following these ancestral precedents in your family's tradition and in the steps of your forebears is perhaps the greatest of Yolŋu virtues.[8]

The idea of following in the steps of ancestors who have gone before is reflected in the Yolŋu concept of *l̲uku* or *djalkiri*. These interchangeable terms effectively describe the Yolŋu system of tenure through which ownership of clan *wäŋa* (homelands), as bestowed by the original ancestors, is normally passed from father to child over successive generations. L̲uku and its synonym djalkiri can be translated into English as 'foot', 'footprint' and 'step', as well as 'root', 'anchor' and 'foundation'.[9] Each homeland has a focal l̲uku site where its founding ancestor entered the *yirralka* (bedrock) and imbued it for all time with the sacred gift of its life-giving märr. Yolŋu clans traditionally define the extent of their larger homelands in terms of the closeness of their lands and waters to these focal l̲uku sites, and do not therefore observe strictly fixed borders between different homelands.

As the Yolŋu legal system for clan homeland tenure, l̲uku is quite literally the foundation of Yolŋu rom. As noted by the anthropologist Franca Tamisari,

> [it] is simultaneously a way of moving through life, coming and going out of being, visiting the same camping places, sitting

> around a hearth which has been used by family members long gone, reproducing or re-performing everyday activities in the right way, and following the way taught and the footprints left by the ancestors.[10]

To say that someone is *l̲uku-ŋupan* (foundation-following) is a way of describing them as a faithful, dependable and responsible person who diligently follows rom, cares for family and participates in ceremonies. The terms *l̲uku-wäŋawuy* (foundation-homeland) and *wäŋa-nhiniŋu* (homeland-living) are the closest to approximating the concept of 'sovereignty' in English.[11] They convey the deep sense of legal authority and autonomy that Yolŋu clans traditionally hold in their ancestral homelands under the dual Yirritja and Dhuwa constitutions. These constitutions are as foundationally important to Yolŋu society as the Australian Constitution is to the Commonwealth's parliamentary democracy.

Homelands are not the only sacred property that Yolŋu clans inherit from their original ancestors. Sealed as inalienable property with each clan homeland is its mad̲ayin. To say that mad̲ayin means 'all things are sacred' is far too simple. Mad̲ayin evokes the deep sacredness of the natural beauty that the original ancestors instilled in the physical world. Everything in the material world is imbued with mad̲ayin because of the natural beauty that the original ancestors instilled into the whole of creation. All things in the physical world are therefore sacred because they are imbued with the mad̲ayin of the original ancestors. All Yolŋu homelands are therefore imbued with this kind of innate and pervasive mad̲ayin.

Where Yolŋu ceremonies are concerned, however, the term maḏayin can also refer to the unique sets of *yäku* (names), *manikay* (songs), *buŋgul* (dances) and *miny'tji* (designs) that clans inherit with each of their homelands. These sacred expressions were recorded by the original ancestors as they first observed and shaped the Yolŋu homelands. Because they describe the deep sacredness of the natural beauty that the original ancestors instilled into the physical world, they form the core content of all clan repertoires performed in ceremonies to this day. These ceremonial sets of names, songs, dances and designs are also considered, in a legal sense, to evidence the ownership of each clan in their ancestral homelands.

Ceremonial participation starts from infancy, because babies are said to crawl with law (rom-gal'-gal'maranhamirri), and dancing in public ceremonies is encouraged as soon as a toddler can walk. Indeed, a desire for ceremonial participation by singing and dancing in the tradition of ancestors is considered by Yolŋu people to be an intrinsically human trait. When a public ceremony is being performed for someone you know, one of the most endearing ways to show them your respect is to dance for them. The term buŋgul (dance) is used synonymously with *garma* (public) ceremonies, while public ceremonial dances themselves are considered a part of the public ceremonial manikay (song) tradition, as they are always performed to accompany corresponding songs.

From a young age, people are expected to learn and identify strongly with the content of their public ceremonial repertoires. If you are in north-east Arnhem Land, for example, and you see a Yolŋu person wearing a T-shirt with a porpoise or shark on it, there is a very good chance that their clothing choice is not random. It would be safe to surmise that the species depicted on their shirt features in the ceremonial names, songs, dances and designs of their homelands, or perhaps in the ceremonial content of another clan to whom they are closely related, such as that of their mother, mother's mother or spouse. Those kinds of close relationships also guide who dances for whom in public ceremonies when someone dances for a clan that is not their own.

Clans consider their sets of ceremonial maḏayin to be unique expressions of their specific ancestral lineages and identities. While all clans are grouped under either the Dhuwa or Yirritja constitution, each clan still maintains its own distinct lineage and identity, like the separate branches of a tree or a river system. This sense of distinctiveness can even extend to different male lineages within larger clans that have primary carriage over a specific clan homeland. In Yolŋu law, these branches are called *ḻikan*, which can be translated into English as 'joint', 'elbow' or 'crescent'.[12]

The ḻikan of any male lineage is an important expression of its sacred connection with ancestors and homelands. A clan's ḻikan commonly represents the ancestral qualities of the ferocious species – saltwater crocodile, for example – from which it overtly traces primary descent. People are encouraged to know and cherish their ḻikan. The ḻikan forms of their ceremonial maḏayin, however, are considered of a more sacred class than those generally performed in public ceremonies.

Manikay or song series typically comprise the greater content of public ceremonies, but strings of deeper ḻikan names are sung at the precise moments when the central ritual actions that give public ceremonies their purposes are executed. These ḻikan name invocations are the same as those called out by the original ancestors when they first observed and shaped the Yolŋu homelands, and impart the legal power and authority of clans to perform binding ceremonial actions directly from their ancestral sources.[13]

Overall, all language sung in ceremonial songs is not considered to be human in origin but, rather, ancestral. Manikay lyrics largely comprise strings of sacred names and archaisms for all things observed, named and recorded by the original ancestors that are found nowhere else in the Yolŋu languages. They are intentionally cryptic and circuitous in nature to allow for ever-deeper layers of meaning to be gleaned from them as people mature throughout their lives.[14]

The dances that accompany ḻikan name invocations are similarly distinctive. The angles and positions in which dancers hold their bent arms are distinctive to the ḻikan of each male lineage and reflect the repeating geometric patterns painted on their corresponding *dhulmu-mulka* (inside-holding) *bathi* (baskets). These sacred baskets are elaborately adorned with feathers and ochre paints. They are the most sacred constructed symbols of clan authority under ancestral law that can be displayed in a public context, and their fabrication and use are strictly controlled by duly trained and authorised ceremonial leaders. When worn hung by a string around the neck in public ceremonies, they vest ancestral power in the wearer.

In initiation and funeral contexts performed in Yolŋu public ceremonies, recipients who are selected to wear sacred baskets are also often painted with *ḻikanbuy* designs. *Ḻikanbuy-wäŋa* (ḻikanbuy places) themselves are consecrated burial grounds. L̲ikanbuy are the most brilliantly elaborate and sacred class of Yolŋu design. They are painted in natural ochre pigments and, again, their application and use are strictly controlled by duly trained and authorised ceremonial leaders. The simplified geometric outlines of these designs, as painted on sacred baskets, are often described as 'raw' in form, while the *bir'yun* (brilliance) of their full l̲ikanbuy renderings are said to be 'cooked'.[15]

In some ways, Yolŋu designs are heraldic in stature and composition. A clan's identity can easily be recognised by the unique shapes, angles and colours of its simplified raw designs. However, those distinctive raw designs can also be emblazoned, supported or crowned with a variety of subjects from a clan's manikay series to form l̲ikanbuy designs. These subjects can take many forms, including plant and animal species, tools, boats, constellations, and cloud and sunset formations. When painted on a ceremonial recipient, they can be readily individualised for the wearer.

By comparison, each Warlpiri homeland in the Tanami Desert is generally represented by a distinctive jukurrpa (dreaming) design that is traditionally burnt into an oval wooden shield. Such shields are publicly displayed in the Kurdiji (Shield) ceremony through which boys are initiated into manhood. Performed by the Parra (Day) and Munga (Night) patri-semimoieties, Kurdiji is the second in the annual cycle of Warlpiri ceremonies. As it begins, women hand their boys over to men for initiation and each is taken to view shields portraying the four different jukurrpa of their warringi (father's father), jinngardi (father's mother), jaja (mother's mother) and jamirdi (mother's father) from each of the four patri-semimoieties.[16] Since 2005, a growing array of these iconic shield designs have been painted onto a row of giant banners that form the backdrop of the main stage at the biennial Milpirri Festival in Lajamanu.[17]

Since the 1950s, l̲ikanbuy designs have formed the foundation of Yolŋu visual art production while retaining their deeply sacred significance as ancestral clan properties. Paintings, sculptures and video art by many noted Yolŋu artists are now exhibited in major art galleries worldwide. Perhaps the most stunning collection of l̲ikanbuy designs by multiple clans in any one work is in the Yirrkala Church Panels of 1962–63. Both standing 3.6 metres high and 1.2 metres wide, these two giant masonite panels were initially painted as an expression of unprecedented cooperation among nine of Yirrkala's resident clans. The l̲ikanbuy designs of six Dhuwa clans are marshalled on the left panel and those of three Yirritja clans on the right panel. When the Australian Government granted a bauxite mining lease over lands surrounding Yirrkala in 1963, the panels became a symbol of Yolŋu solidarity against this intrusion. They were presented to the Methodist missionaries who administrated the town at Yirrkala and were initially hung either side of the crucifix inside the Yirrkala Church to demonstrate the equality of Yolŋu and Christian faiths.[18] They now hang on public display in the Mulka Museum at Yirrkala.

The Yolŋu educator and lead singer of Yothu Yindi, Mandawuy Yunupiŋu, described how, when he was a young boy, his father, Mungurrawuy, painted Gumatj clan l̲ikanbuy designs onto the Yirritja panel:

> My father was kind in accepting the non-Aboriginal people who came to him. He also wanted to bring into the church his law, and I think I inherit that sense of balance from him. He wanted to give non-Aboriginal people, even the missionaries, a sense of 'Hey listen, we've been here a long time and this is what we know. This is our way of telling you that we go deeper, and our layers of knowledge go deeper than you thought.' His paintings on the right panel are of the *Saltwater Crocodile*, the Maralitja man, and the *Yellow Ochre* man, Wirrili, from Biranybirany, the same land where the *Saltwater Crocodile* discovered fire. He used my hair [as a brush] for that painting, so it's very significant and historic for me.[19]

Later in 1963, the striking presence of these dual panels in the Yirrkala Church inspired the painted borders of the much smaller Yirrkala Bark Petitions, which were sent to the Australian House of Representatives to assert Yolŋu sovereignty over their homelands and protest the proposed mine. While unsuccessful with regard to sovereignty, they prompted an ensuing series of similar petitions that have culminated in calling for a treaty between Indigenous peoples and the Australian Government and a constitutional Voice to Parliament for Indigenous Australians. The Wuyal Petition of 1968 succeeded in retaining the traditional Yolŋu name of Nhulunbuy over the new mining town near Yirrkala, but the greater calls of the Barunga Statement in 1988, the Elcho Island and Yirrkala Petitions in 1998, the East Arnhem Land Petition in 2008, and the Uluru Statement from the Heart in 2017 have yet to be realised.[20]

GOVERNANCE AND RESPONSIBILITY

Michael Jakamara Nelson's *Possum and Wallaby Dreaming* design for the forecourt of Australia's Parliament House was deliberately created to show how the representational and legislative work of the building can be equated with the Warlpiri systems of law and governance that have long functioned in the Tanami Desert. Just as Parliament House is a formal place of meeting, debate and decision-making for elected officials from throughout Australia, *Possum and Wallaby Dreaming* shows how the annual Jardiwarnpa ceremony brings people of all four Warlpiri patri-semimoieties, representing their myriad homelands across the Tanami Desert, to meet, debate and make decisions as a composite body of polity and government structure.

Displayed inside Parliament House are other formal representations and declarations of Indigenous polities and government structures. Hanging near the 1963 Yirrkala Bark Petitions and the 1968 Wuyal Petition is the Barunga Statement of 1988. This was the first call on the Australian Government to enter a formal treaty with the Indigenous owners and occupiers of Australia in recognition of their pre-existing sovereignty and human rights. Again, the Barunga Statement is bordered by painted designs. Those on the left were painted by the late Yolŋu leader G Yunupiŋu and marshal the l̲ikanbuy designs of four closely related Yirritja clans, while the painting on the right by Arrernte leader Wenten Rubuntja depicts a prevalent Two Sisters altyerrenge that connects the ancestral law of many different groups across the vast distances of Australia's deserts.

Indigenous bodies of polity cover the whole of Australia and stretch across vast geographical regions spanning multiple language groups. While natural boundaries such as gulfs and mountain ranges sometimes separated neighbouring regions, ancient trade routes nonetheless spanned the Australian continent, such as the ancient Emu trade route traditionally walked to connect Warlpiri people in the Tanami Desert with the Kimberley coastline.[21]

Before the First Fleet founded the Colony of New South Wales at Sydney Cove on 26 January 1788, Indigenous bodies of polity held the only governmental structures to exist in Australia. While their borders are only loosely defined and generally unimportant in Indigenous property laws, their reach is largely demarcated by a combination of intersecting traits, including their regional natural environments, their overarching systems of social organisation and their distinctive traditional styles of ceremonial song, dance and design. While generically characterised as 'songlines' in Aboriginal English, these many distinct regional styles of public ceremonial song and dance include *kab kar* from East Torres Strait, *na* from West Torres Strait, Wik-Mungkan *apalech* from West Cape York, Yolŋu manikay from north-east Arnhem Land, *kun-borrk* from West Arnhem Land, *yoi* from the Tiwi Islands, Warlpiri *purlapa* from the Tanami Desert, and A̲nangu *inma* from the Central Desert.

Over the past two centuries, many of these distinct regional song-and-dance styles have become critically endangered. Discriminatory Crown policies, the geographical expansion of commercial agriculture and mining, bloody massacres, and forced removals of Indigenous people from their homelands and families have threatened the continuity of these traditions to varying degrees in different regions. Assimilationist education and administrative systems aimed at erasing Indigenous law and governance structures have worsened this situation, as has political inaction in response to repeated calls for a treaty between Indigenous peoples and the Australian Government. Since the 1970s, ethnomusicologists and linguists have played particularly vital roles in supporting Indigenous communities to maintain their traditions despite the immense challenges. Today, growing numbers of Indigenous ethnomusicologists and linguists are working tirelessly to ensure their own regional traditions are fully functional.[22]

Yet Indigenous bodies of polity and government structures nonetheless endure in Australia. A detailed account of the typical legal responsibilities and citizen protections they afford is offered in the text of the Elcho Island and Yirrkala Petitions of 1998:

> Letter to the Parliament of the Commonwealth of Australia on traditional Yolŋu Law.
>
> We, the undersigned, are *d̠alkarra* and *djirrikay* (the political representatives and leaders) of our sovereign clan/nations comprising all the Yolŋu (Aboriginal people) within this Miwatj region of North-East Arnhem Land.
>
> We bring to you our diplomatic request from: the *Ŋärra'*/ traditional Parliaments of our clan/nation estates to: the Parliament of the Commonwealth of Australia.
>
> We request that you recognise:
>
> 1. the *Dhulmu-mulka Bathi* (Title Deeds) which establish the legal tenure for each of our traditional clan estates. Your Westminster system calls this Native Title.

2. the jurisdiction of our *Ŋärra'*/Traditional Parliament in the same way as we recognise your Parliament and Westminster system of Government.
3. both formally and legally recognise our *Maḏayin* system of law. Within our *Maḏayin* there are three different levels of Government that provide for the peace, order and good government of the people/citizens:
   i. Open or public [*Garma*] ceremonies where all citizens may be present;
   ii. Semi-Public [*Dhuni'*] chambers of law where only certain parts of the legal procedures may be conducted in public;
   iii. Closed/restricted [*Ŋärra'*] chambers of law which may only be attended by those political leaders who represent the citizens.

The colonisation of this land and the imposition of a foreign system of law has not prevented Yolŋu from holding, maintaining and continuing to assent to our traditional system of law. This is our Common Law right which the High Court of Australia has partially recognised. As citizens, our rights must be protected at law.

In 1967 the Commonwealth of Australia belatedly recognised our citizenship of this land, Australia. However, we were already citizens of this land, recognised by our *Maḏayin*.

In the face of many imposed obstacles and pressures, we still continue to educate our children and future leaders, manage our estates, engage in economic and diplomatic exchanges between clans/nations, discipline offenders, care for our sick and elderly and practice hospitality to foreigners who live on or visit our *yirralka* (estates [bedrock]).

There must be dialogue between the two systems of law because Yolŋu law, like your law, is based on the key principles of *mäwaya* (peace and justice), *dhapirrk* (consistency between different levels of law) and *wana-lupthun* (the assent of the *rom-waṯaŋu walal*/citizens to those laws).

We extend to you, the Honourable Leaders of the Commonwealth of Australia, our invitation to come to a meeting where we can discuss these issues in much greater depth so that together we can forge a partnership of co-operation and dialogue based on mutual trust and respect for each other's law. Without this recognition we will live in perpetual dependence in this land that is ours by birthright, silenced and oppressed by a foreign system of law.

Presented to the Prime Minister, the Hon. John Howard MHR, at Yirrkala on 27 February 1998 on behalf of the following clan/nations of the Miwatj region:

Rirratjiŋu, Gumatj, Gälpu, Madarrpa, Djapu', Maŋgalili, Marrakulu, Munyuku, Dhalwaŋu, Dhudi-Djapu', Wangurri, Dätiwuy, Ŋaymil, Djambarrpuyŋu, Warramiri, Golumala, Ritharrŋu, Marraŋu, Dhäpuyŋu, Gupapuyŋu, Djarrwark.

The Elcho Island and Yirrkala Petitions present a very clear snapshot of what Yolŋu leaders consider to constitute good governance and legal consistency. They outline that Yolŋu law is based on key principles of *mäwaya* (peace and justice) and *dhapirrk* (evenness, order and consistency), and the assent to law of all Yolŋu citizens as rom-waṯaŋu (law-holders). It asserts the rights of Yolŋu people under the foundational yirralka laws of their own homelands to educate their children and future leaders, manage their estates, engage in diplomacy and economic exchanges among Yolŋu clans and with other entities, discipline offenders, care for the sick and elderly, and welcome foreigners. These kinds of fundamental legal protections and responsibilities are found as hallmarks of good governance and legal consistency within all Indigenous bodies in Australia.[23]

The Elcho Island and Yirrkala Petitions also explain that Yolŋu law provides for three different levels of government that are enacted through three different levels of ceremonial performance. These three levels of governance through ceremonies, in order of openness to restrictedness, are commonly known as garma, *dhuni'* and *ŋärra'*. The *Yolŋu Knowledge Constitution*, painted in 2002 by the Yolŋu leader and academic Joe Neparrŋa Gumbula (Figures 7, 8 and 9), shows how they are organised (see it in colour on the inside back cover of this book).[24] The bottom half of the diagram, coloured green, represents the garma (public) level of government that is enacted through open ceremonies where all citizens, including children, can be present. All formal manikay (song) and buŋgul (dance) elements performed openly in ceremonies, including the corresponding miny'tji (designs) worn by performers, are inherently garma, and participation through

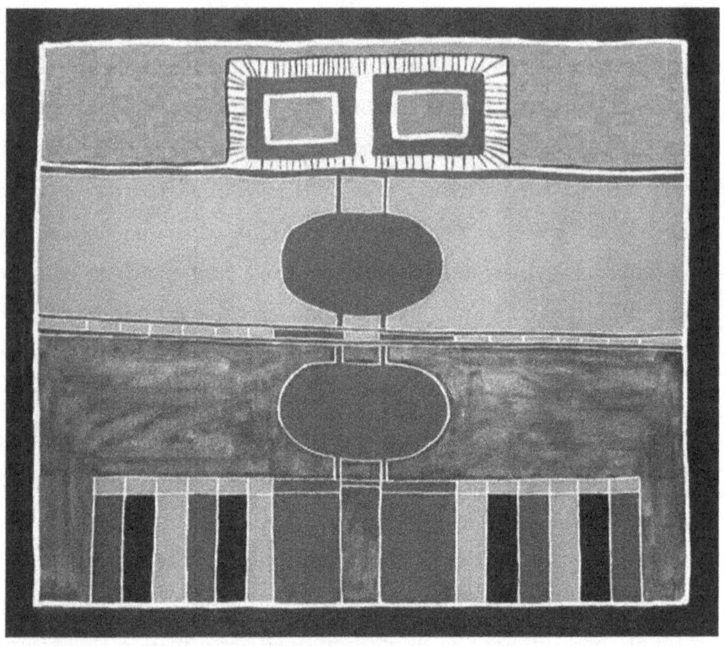

FIGURE 7: Joe Neparrŋa Gumbula, *Yolŋu Knowledge Constitution*, 2002. This painting shows the organisation of the three levels of Yolŋu governance.

dancing is encouraged from infancy. A wide array of legal processes are enacted through garma ceremonies, including the initiation of boys into bachelorhood, healing and palliative care, extensive funeral and purification rites, diplomatic exchanges between clans and resolving disputes and disciplining offenders.[25]

It is important to understand, however, that these processes are not uniformly performed as public ceremonies by other groups in Australia. By contrast, in the Warlpiri context, song-and-dance series of the purlapa style, which are performed predominantly by men, and of the *yuwalyu* style, performed by women, are often enacted as public ceremonies but children do not traditionally dance in them. Of the annual cycle of Warlpiri ceremonies, only the Jardiwarnpa fire purification ceremony and the beginning of the Kurdiji ceremony, when women hand their boys over to men for initiation, are presented in public.[26]

The top half of Gumbula's diagram is divided into two layers, coloured yellow above the middle and red at the top, that respectively represent the dhuni' (sheltered) and ŋärra' (restricted) levels of government. The Elcho Island and Yirrkala Petitions describe the ŋärra' level of government as a traditional Yolŋu parliament. However, plans for binding legal decisions to be made by senior men in secluded ŋärra' ceremonies must be rendered open to discussion beforehand and subsequent review in the enveloping dhuni' context of the *riyawarra* (verification) ground, where women and children await them.

The ŋärra' ceremony is an important legal chamber in which jural decisions are seriously discussed and made binding. Once a ŋärra' ceremony is over, all men in attendance return to the riyawarra ground to communicate outcomes and perform a concluding dhuni' ceremony with their female counterparts. All citizens, including children, can be present. To conclude this dhuni' ceremony, participants may choose to show their assent by walking into the sea together in a final purifying act called *wa<u>n</u>a-<u>l</u>upthun* (arm-washing). This staged process of decision-making through linked dhuni' and ŋärra' ceremonies is a bicameral parliamentary system, with two legislative chambers, and the legal decisions made through it are its binding acts of parliament.[27]

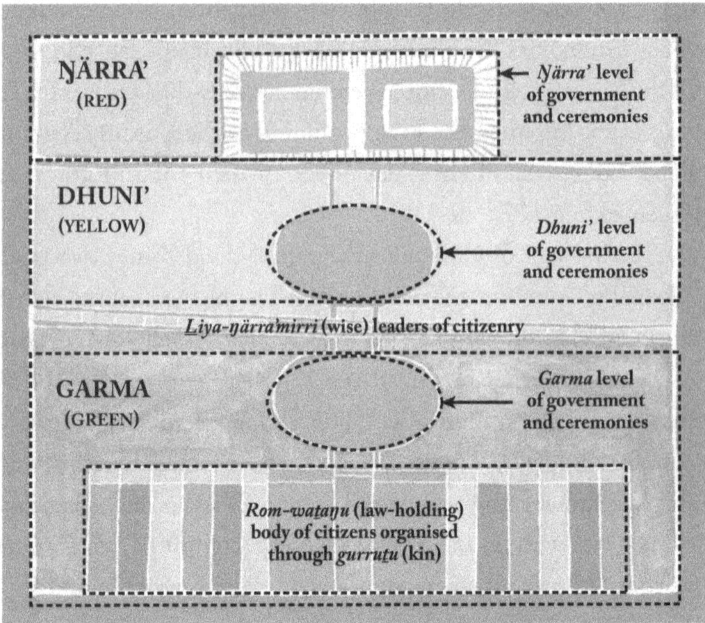

FIGURE 8: Yolŋu governance ascends through three levels of ceremonies of varying degrees of openness, ranging from garma (most open) to ŋärra' (most restricted). Ceremonies are led by the liya-ŋärra'mirri, seen here as a band between the garma and dhuni' levels.

All dhulmu-mulka bathi (inside-holding baskets), and all sung invocations of *likan yäku* (joining names) and their corresponding dances are inherently dhuni'. Innermost knowledge of the original ancestors themselves and their luku (foundation) sites is inherently ŋärra' and not normally communicated outside closed ceremonial contexts. However, all citizens may request to have this knowledge fully explained to them before they pass away.[28]

At the most senior level of government, all Yolŋu clans are led by their *d̲ilak* (elders), who hold ultimate responsibility and authority to make binding legal decisions. The d̲ilak are also ultimately responsible for training and appointing qualified ceremonial leaders who can prepare and direct complex public ceremonies in their entirety. Leaders with this expertise and authority are generally considered *l̲iya-ŋärra'mirri* (wise). They are represented by the thin horizontal yellow band that separates the garma and dhuni' sections of Gumbula's diagram. The terms d̲alkarramirri and *djirrikaymirr* are also specifically attributed to mature men, respectively of Yirritja and Dhuwa clans, who are trained to lead public ceremonies and are authorised to sing l̲ikan yäku invocations on behalf of their clans.[29]

The burden of duty upon such Indigenous elders and ceremonial leaders is immense. As seniority in Indigenous law grows, so too do responsibilities to provide, negotiate and arbitrate on behalf of other citizens. Ultimately, Indigenous elders and ceremonial leaders are responsible for upholding ancestral law. They are responsible for continuing their people's traditions, maintaining peace and social order, and sustaining workable relationships with related groups, while simultaneously negotiating newer challenges and opportunities across a much wider array of present-day governmental, commercial, educational and other interests.

OBLIGATIONS AND PROTECTIONS

The Yolŋu legal system provides people and the environment with a comprehensive variety of standards and protections, including protections for the full ownership rights of each Yolŋu clan in its ancestral homelands. These are inherited through male lineages and include fully integrated ownership protections for the unique sets of ceremonial names, songs, dances and designs that clans inherit with each of their homelands. However, while Yolŋu people inherit their clan homelands and ceremonies though their male lineages, various other rights in the homelands and ceremonies of related clans, including those of enjoyment and potential succession, are passed down through female lineages (Figure 9).

Gumbula's *Yolŋu Knowledge Constitution* diagram shows how these relational networks are structured. Its horizontal mirroring represents the equality in Yolŋu society of intermarrying clans under the dual Yirritja and Dhuwa constitutions (Figure 9). The two brown vertical lines that connect all three levels of Yolŋu governance represent the *yarraṯa* (string) or male lineage that respectively runs in each Yirritja and Dhuwa clan. This carries the legal authority and full ownership of each clan in its homelands and ceremonies. These clans are nonetheless bound together into a functioning Yolŋu society by equally important relationships that run through female lineages.

Female lineages create networks of relationships that link everyone in every clan to every other clan in their social sphere. As enabled by Yolŋu adoption law, everyone who engages in Yolŋu society will usually have a place in this expansive system of *gurruṯu* (relationships), whether they were born Yolŋu or not. This ensures that all social engagements, whether with close family or newcomers, are conducted respectfully in keeping with ancestral law. Consequently, all people in the Yolŋu gurruṯu system are descended

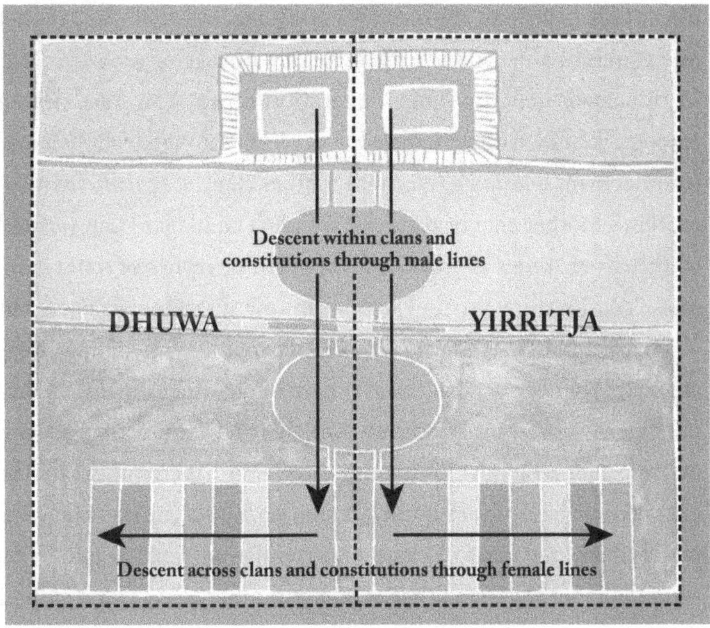

FIGURE 9: Equality between the dual Yirritja and Dhuwa constitutions is reflected in the left–right mirroring of Joe Gumbula's painting. Together with legal and familial lineages traced through male and female lines (vertical and horizontal arrows respectively), this system maintains balance in Yolŋu society.

through the male line of their own clans but can be related to as many as twenty-four other clans through female lineages. In Gumbula's diagram, the two long segmented rectangles that run horizontally along its bottom border plot how these female lineages work in principle.[30]

Yolŋu people effectively recognise three parallel female lineages through which they trace their relationships to other clans: their own direct female lineage, the direct female lineage of their *bäpa* (father) one generation up, and the direct female lineage of *gäthu* (children in their own male line) one generation down. You trace descent through your own direct female lineage back through your *ŋäṉḏipulu* (mother clan), *märipulu* (mother's mother clan), *wakupulu* (mother's mother's mother clan or recursive woman's child clan) and *yapapulu* (mother's mother's mother's mother clan or recursive sister clan). These relationships also flow to heirs in your direct female lineage via your own children, if you are female, and your sister's children, if you are male. Your bäpa and gäthu also have female lineages of their own, parallel to yours, that are exactly like this and extend your network of important relationships to even more clans. The mother's mother clan of your bäpa, for example, is your *gäthupulu* (man's child clan), which forms the basis of close and friendly relations in family and ceremonial settings, while the mother's mother clan of your gäthu is that of a man's *milmara* (betrothed) *mukul rumaru* (mother-in-law). When a woman marries, her mother-in-law will instead be a *mukul bäpa* (aunt) from a yapapulu.

People typically inherit standing access to the homelands and ceremonial expressions of their ŋäṉḏipulu and mature adults can become experienced *djuŋgayi* (arbiters) for the clans of their mothers. Experienced senior djuŋgayi stand in a binding legal relationship with their mother clans. This role tasks djuŋgayi with working for their mother clans by either approving or vetoing legal decisions they may seek to take, assisting in arbitrating their disputes and ensuring the correctness of their ceremonial actions as expressions of ancestral law. The *yothu-yindi* or child–mother relationship bridges both the Dhuwa and Yirritja patrimoieties or constitutions of Yolŋu law. As marriages always involve people of a clan from each patrimoiety and children are always born into the constitution opposite their mother, children make for the perfect arbiters of their mother clans' interests. Children are the immediate descendants of their mother clans but, being born into the constitution opposite their mother, can never become full inheritors or owners of their mothers' homelands and ceremonies.[31]

A full ownership transfer between two different clans can only happen when they are incorporated under the same constitution. In those instances, the two clans concerned need to be either both Yirritja or both Dhuwa. The usual pathway to a succession of this kind reaches back one additional generation along the female line. If you were descended from a märipulu (mother's mother clan) that had no direct male heirs of its own, then you would likely be in a strong legal position to secure full ownership of its homelands and ceremonies for your own clan. In fact, clans will often appoint specific people as stewards from among their women's daughters' children and task them with learning all their law to ensure that those potential lines of succession are well embedded and broadly recognised.

Though less common, a full ownership transfer can also occur between two different clans under the same constitution who recognise each other as a yapapulu of equal social standing. Technically, a yapapulu is a clan that is four generations removed from your own as either a mother's mother's mother's mother clan or a woman's daughter's daughter's daughter's children's clan. A yapapulu relationship is not naturally close and familiar like the one you would have with your märipulu, and you would normally seek a yapapulu's permission before entering their homelands or performing combined ceremonies with them. Yapapulu relationships can be strengthened and made closer, however, when diplomacy ceremonies are performed in their honour. Betrothal ceremonies between a man and his intended mukul rumaru (mother-in-law) also happen between two different clans under the same constitution, and can similarly work to strengthen relationships between them.[32]

SHARING AND ALLIANCES

Legally binding alliances between clans under the same constitution who identify each other as märipulu (mother's mother clan), yapapulu (sister clan), gäthupulu (man's child clan), and milmara (betrothed) via a man's mukul rumaru (mother-in-law) enable all ceremonies to reliably function in Yolŋu society. These clan alliances or federations are commonly called *reŋgitj* in the Yolŋu languages, which technically means 'body', but in the sense of a body corporate or, to be precise, a body comprising constituent member clans:

> *Reŋgitj* primarily refers to a place on a group's country where ancestral beings emerged to commence or gathered to continue their journey across the land. These places are often characterised by particular geographical features or botanical images which iconicly [*sic*] convey ideas of connection between groups. For instance, the creeks or tributaries formed by the water flowing

> into a river, the rays radiating out from the sun, parallel paths cut through the shrubbery along a beach, or the branches of a tree departing from its trunk are examples of *reŋgitj* places ... The creeks, paths or branches are said to represent the different groups which are distributed along the same ancestral trajectory.
>
> *Reŋgitj* places ... are like embassies which represent and stand for different groups on another group's country. It is at these *reŋgitj* places that the ancestors 'picked up all the names' which were to be distributed along their journey. Thus the *reŋgitj*, as a visible mark or imprint on the land, is characterised as a place of origin, the repository of all the names, as well as a kind of mapped visual expression of the connection between people and places which is to be carried out in the temporal sequence of the journey. In fact, it is through the movement of the ancestral body over the land that the connections embodied in the *reŋgitj* place are realised and the names distributed.[33]

The knowledge generated in reŋgitj ceremonial contexts is considered the most definitive. In this sense, the overall quality of a ceremony is indexical to the number of people who gather to participate in it, and the greater the number of clans present, the more definitive the knowledge generated there will be. People will accordingly explain the credentials of their knowledge by referring to the various reŋgitj contexts through which they acquired it.[34] Reŋgitj ceremonies are also contexts in which disagreements and divisions must be resolved or put aside before such knowledge can be shared and combined ceremonies can be undertaken in common purpose.[35]

Each clan's ownership rights in its own homelands commonly stop at the yirralka (bedrock), with all rights to subsurface resources being owned corporately by reŋgitj alliances comprising multiple clans. All decisions relating to the subsurface, such as mining negotiations, must therefore be made by the reŋgitj alliance collectively. Similarly, when full ownership rights in a homeland are transferred from one clan to another, they will normally flow to another clan within the same reŋgitj alliance.[36] In some cases, attaining new rights to a homeland within a reŋgitj alliance will not be predicated on conventional succession laws but, rather, be granted to an individual leader and their heirs in return for long and exemplary service in mounting joint ceremonies.

Small reŋgitj sites are also encapsulated within larger homelands, and function like embassies. It is protocol for visitors of a clan's homeland to initially stop upon entry to a reŋgitj site that, due to its shared ancestral significance, has been designated for their own clan. There, the visitors will light a signalling fire before either seeking out the homeland's owners or, if matters are tense, awaiting their arrival.[37]

Reŋgitj as a legal concept evokes common themes of confluence, shared ancestry, accord, cooperation and political alliance among different member clans and a body of people bound by shared heritage under a common waŋarr (ancestor). Established reŋgitj alliances with other clans are typically referenced in a clan's manikay series.[38] However, reŋgitj alliances with new clans, based on evidence of shared ancestry, can be brokered through new ceremonial exchanges.[39] When strings of l̲ikan names are sung at decisive moments in public ceremonies, they are accompanied throughout by a fast and commanding *reŋgitj bilma* (clapsticks) pattern that brings together all participants in unity and signals ancestral significance and legal weight.[40]

In its broadest sense, reŋgitj is the recognition and realisation that all people of different clans under a common constitution ultimately share common ancestry and a common system of law. It is as much about the act of sharing as what is shared. The burden of duty on Yolŋu elders and ceremonial leaders to maintain high-functioning reŋgitj alliances is immense, as the weighty responsibilities of upholding ancestral law, continuing ancestral traditions, maintaining peace and order, sustaining ceremonial partnerships and negotiating a plethora of emerging challenges and opportunities ultimately relies on their fair and cooperative approaches to decision-making.

5

FAMILY BUSINESS

Marriage is not the same in every society, nor are the ways we understand family relationships. Yet in every human language there are terms to identify different relatives in our families, whether they be close or distant. Terms like husband and wife, grandmother and grandfather, mother and father, brother and sister, uncle and aunt, cousins and in-laws are typically mapped by anthropologists when they seek to understand family structures, or kinship. Kinship in families also unlocks understanding of property law and leadership structures in Australian Indigenous societies, as descent and birth order inform who inherits what in a family, whether it be an ancestral homeland or leadership responsibilities.

There are several big differences between Indigenous kinship systems in Australia and those brought here by the English. For example, in Indigenous societies across Australia in the customary systems, children will simply refer to their mother and all of their mother's sisters as *mother*. Sometimes they will also identify their *big mothers*, who are older, and *little mothers*, who are younger. The idea of who is related to you also extends beyond biological relationships, as kinship terms are commonly applied to anyone you might know or meet, and even to ancestral beings and the homelands they inhabit. To hear someone say, 'That's my mother's mother' upon seeing a photo of a whale, for example, is a fairly common occurrence, as people do not traditionally distinguish between their human relatives and the species to whom they are ancestrally linked. After all, all living humans are merely physical manifestations of eternal ancestral beings who can usually assume both human forms and those of other species. If there are kinship systems anywhere in the world as complex as those of Indigenous cultures in Australia, we are not aware of them.

Even though there are various Indigenous kinship systems in Australia, there is remarkable similarity among them. One of the most common old traditions across Australia was that, as men grew older, they were allowed to have more than one wife. Most young men once aspired to have more than one wife, as the more wives he had, the more socially powerful he could become. In most Indigenous societies across Australia, babies were betrothed at birth to those they could marry according to kinship law, though this did not mean those marriages necessarily took place. This arrangement would ensure, however, that the betrothed couple would always be deemed husband and wife in a sacred sense, as predetermined by ancestral law, even if they did not marry. They would treat each other respectfully, with a gentle humour and special friendship marking their lifelong bond.

Men had to earn the right to a wife by giving gifts to her parents and demonstrating he was a suitable husband who could provide for and bring prestige to the family, so that any children would have a secure place in the world. Usually, a man's first wife was much older than him and his treatment of her was a critical factor in the willingness of other families to marry their daughters to him. While average numbers of wives varied in different regions across Australia, men with many wives were held in high regard for having demonstrated their worthiness this way. Some men still marry more than one wife in this traditional way, though this is far less common than it used to be.

Indigenous legal systems always have fundamental rules that govern not just marriage but all relationships. Yolŋu society in north-east Arnhem Land, for example, is organised around the balanced coexistence of two equal constitutions of ancestral law called Dhuwa and Yirritja. As introduced in Chapter 3, there are some sixty Yolŋu clans; roughly half are Dhuwa and the other half are Yirritja. Yolŋu society rests upon their cooperation through intermarriage in each generation. All Yolŋu children have both a Dhuwa parent and a Yirritja parent, thereby ensuring this balance. This immutable sense of relatedness extends not only to people but also to anything else with a name, including clan homelands themselves and the various species and ancestors who inhabit them. Such is the patterning of the world established by the original ancestors in all of their living manifestations, including all humans and all other species of their descent.

Elsewhere, in some desert societies, moieties only have relative names, but everyone knows to which moiety they belong and whom they can marry. What is important about this aspect of Indigenous law is that everyone must marry someone from the correct moiety. This rule is sacrosanct and to breach it is to condemn yourself to ostracism and strife. Such marriage laws are regarded as gifts from the ancestors, originating in the sacred past as fundamental rules that all should follow. Christian missionaries, law-making authorities and government officials in Australia went to great lengths to prevent Indigenous people from following these laws and marrying according to tradition. Colonisation, missionaries, removals and incarceration on reserves forced Indigenous people to adapt their kinship systems in ways that helped them survive and maintain their connections to homelands. Holding families together and maintaining ancestral connections has required great ingenuity, especially in the face of harsh and often brutal colonial and assimilation policies.

To ensure that young Yolŋu people are reminded of the importance of traditional marriage law, the late David Gulpilil Dalaythŋu[1] collaborated with filmmakers Rolf de Heer and Peter Djigirr to make the film *Ten Canoes*, which won a Special Jury Prize at the 2006 Cannes Festival. This was not their first collaboration, but it was one that Gulpilil initiated and a story he had wanted to tell for many years.[2]

Gulpilil had the right qualifications and knowledge to tell this complex story as he was born and raised in the traditions shown in the film. His birth was recorded by missionaries in July 1953 in Arnhem Land, where he was born on his father's homeland, Gulpilil, for which he was named. He was raised by his parents in the Yolŋu world, which was then untouched by outsiders, speaking his mother's and father's languages, Ganalbiŋu and Manydjalpiŋu. He saw a White person for the first time as a child when a plane landed in his country, and became a man having thoroughly learnt his people's traditions, especially through his commitment to ceremonies. He excelled as a dancer, and in his youth was acknowledged by his own people as one of the greatest. He was agile, powerful and graceful in his ceremonial performances.

Gulpilil attended school in Maningrida where, in 1969, the British filmmaker Nicolas Roeg was scouting locations for his second film, *Walkabout*.[3] He saw Gulpilil dancing and promptly cast him in the role of an Aboriginal youth who rescues two White children whose father has committed suicide, and leads them to safety through the desert. His charisma and youthful physicality charmed the world and he became a national and international celebrity. Children learnt about the magic of Indigenous relationships with nature by watching his next film, *Storm Boy*, which cemented him as a great Australian actor.[4]

TEN CANOES

Working with Gulpilil and his colleagues who reside in the community of Ramangin̲iŋ (Ramingining) in Arnhem Land, Rolf de Heer wove a complex story visually and intellectually in *Ten Canoes*. The film depicts the polygynous marriage institution and the bloody retribution exacted when tensions are ignited in the form of a sorcerer who threatens the peace and good order of a community with his otherness and distance. Gulpilil knew well that these characteristics of the sorcerer represented the tensions exacerbated by the closeness and distance of marriage and alliance between clans, both genealogically and geographically.[5] The film's synopsis explains that:

> Ridjimiraril lived with his three wives, wise Banalandju, jealous Nowalingu and beautiful young Munandjarra, in a camp with others, including Birrinbirrin, the fat honey man who always ate too much. Some distance away, in the single men's camp, lived Yeeralparil, Ridjimiraril's younger brother. Yeeralparil had no wives yet, and none promised, but he was keen on that beautiful Munandjarra, who he felt should be his. He would always make excuses to be near Ridjimiraril's camp, in the hope of catching a glimpse of her.[6]

The film is set in both the present day and the ancestral past. The character of the Storyteller, played by Gulpilil, narrates the English metanarrative, while the character of Minygululu, played by Peter Minygululu, tells a story of a trip taken by ten men to harvest bark to make canoes in his own language, Ganalbiŋu.

Ramangiṉiŋ is a town of about 800 Yolŋu people in central Arnhem Land, created in the early 1970s when the mission of Miliŋinbi became overcrowded. This meant that Yolŋu people from different areas came to live together, sometimes long distances from their traditional lands. There are about sixteen clans speaking about eight different dialects living in Ramangiṉiŋ today.

Stretching south and east of the town is the Arafura Swamp, a large area of freshwater wetlands. The Arafura Swamp is a border zone between the Yolŋu people of north-east Arnhem Land, including the Ritharrŋu and Ganalbiŋu clans, and the neighbouring groups of western Arnhem Land, such as the Kunwinjku. It extends to 130,000 hectares during the wet season and is home to an incredible variety of bird, plant and animal life, including possibly the largest biomass of crocodiles in the world. *Ten Canoes* reconstructs scenes based on photographs of canoeists taken by Donald Thomson, a University of Melbourne anthropologist who worked in Arnhem Land in the mid-1930s, when only a few Europeans had ventured there.[7]

Men and women formed exchange partnerships with people of distant groups, and polygynous men occupied nodes in the exchange network through the obligations of their many daughters' husbands, as well as their own obligations, to their wives' kin. *Marradjiri* exchange and diplomacy ceremonies provided occasions for trade between distant groups.

Except for Gulpilil, who had been working in feature films for forty years, this was the first experience of acting for the cast of *Ten Canoes*. In keeping with the idea that living Yolŋu people follow in the steps of their ancestors, actors in the film's present-day bark-harvesting sequences also played the roles of the ancestors. The preparations for making the film involved the construction of canoes, or *lipalipa*, and they, too, play a major role in the story.

The plot revolves around the Indigenous institution of polygynous marriage and the associated institution of levirate marriage.[8] Polygyny is the technical term for the practice of a man having more than one wife at the same time, which is the most common form of polygamy, or plural marriage, overall. Levirate marriage is the practice of a widow marrying her deceased husband's brother. Such marriage arrangements are very formal institutions in Indigenous societies. The plot also involves alliance, betrothal, wife-raiding, sorcery, retribution and the institution of makarraṯa, the ceremony in which armed men execute revenge and settle disputes. This ritualised form of punishment and retribution was made famous by WEH Stanner in his Boyer Lectures on ABC Radio in the 1960s.[9] As the film unfolds, we are treated to the workings of the reŋgitj alliance system found in Yolŋu society and the makarraṯa ceremony, hence the film's advertising slogan: '10 canoes, 150 spears and 3 wives'. The members of the aggrieved clan throw spears at the accused culprit until blood is drawn. As de Heer had learnt:

> Sometimes the wound is fatal, sometimes only minor. Occasionally a partner is chosen by the culprit, and both face the spears. Justice is

> deemed to be done when either one, the innocent or the perceived guilty, is hit. In many areas payback has been further refined to be a simple close-range spearing of the culprit in the leg.[10]

Dayindi, played by Gulpilil's son Jamie Gulpilil, had been seen glancing at the youngest wife of his brother, and in such a small residential grouping, behaviour like this rarely goes unnoticed. Thus, his much older brother, Minygululu, relates a story to him concerning a man like himself, Yeeralparil, who coveted the wife of his brother Ridjimiraril. Minygululu's story is told over several days during the expedition into the Arafura wetlands as a parable instructing his younger brother on the consequences of his behaviour. As de Heer's synopsis explains:

> Ten men, led by old Minygululu, head into the forest to harvest barks for canoe making. It is the season of goose egg gathering, and the men are looking forward to getting out onto the swamp and hunting the magpie geese and their eggs. Minygululu learns that young Dayindi, on his first goose egg hunting expedition, has taken a fancy to Minygululu's third and youngest wife. Tribal [Traditional] law is in danger of being broken: Minygululu decides to deal with the situation by telling Dayindi an ancestral story, a story that will take a very long time to tell, all through the next days of canoe making and swamp travelling and goose egg gathering.[11]

CANOES IN CULTURE

Canoes often appear in ancestral law. The Seven Sisters, for example, whose travels are memorialised in the Pleiades constellation, travel in a canoe as they move in advance of a pursuing suitor. The canoe represents institutions that nurture society, such as polygyny, the levirate, and the genealogical and geographical scales involved in marriage alliances.

The Pleiades constellation, although difficult to see with the naked eye, is visible from most places in the world. Pitjantjatjara women perform a special dance in their own Seven Sisters ceremony that shows how to move your head to see the constellation in the night sky. The constellation is celebrated in ancestral law across Australia. Academic Christine Judith Nicholls refers to it as:

> … [T]he most defining and predominant meta-narratives chronicled in ancient mainland Australia – the story of a predatory, lascivious, rejected loner – an Ancestral Being initially in the guise of a man – who relentlessly pursues seven sisters (Ancestral Women) over land and sky.
>
> … [It] begins in Martu country in the west (the Pilbara region) … In hot pursuit, the man travels east, crossing the Ngaanyatjarra lands in WA and the Pitjantjatjara and Yankunytjara country on the APY (A̲n̲angu, Pitjantjatjara and Yankunytjara) lands in South Australia. By this time, the seven sisters have become stars … (Subsequently, the man takes the form of Orion's Belt.)

> ... [In Warlpiri law,] the seven sisters become the Napaljarri-warnu and their pursuer, in one of his shape-shifting iterations, a Wardilyka (Bush Turkey).[12]

This great metanarrative of male lust and female autonomy is also celebrated in north-east Arnhem Land, where the Seven Sisters travel by canoe. Their journey from Arnhem Land takes them southwards, and their many storied adventures are celebrated all the way down to the South Australian coast. Such themes are apt in the environments of Arnhem Land, where people have travelled along the coastlines and wetlands by canoe for thousands of years. While in the human world, those who travel together in canoes are men; in the spiritual world, the canoe is inhabited by a group of sisters supported by the levirate, but pursued by a suitor who wants them all as his wives. In this way, the canoe represents the tensions of the polygynous nature of marriage and the common fate of sisters. It also symbolises the strength of the marriage institution, founded in the ancestral past, in determining the fate of present-day human society.

ANCIENT INSTITUTIONS

The film *Ten Canoes* provided an opportunity for its cast and the community members involved to explore their ancient institutions and practices, many of which had declined during the mission era but were being reclaimed through new creative initiatives like this film. It cannot be accidental that the film's plot structure – based in the tensions of levirate marriage – revolves around the canoe expedition undertaken by the men. In so doing, it reveals, perhaps unintentionally, the extraordinary tensions that emerge in marriage alliance systems when distant and faraway groups are involved in obtaining wives, whether by betrothal or abduction. Several major themes in Indigenous society, particularly those of this area in Arnhem Land, emerge through the plot and structure of *Ten Canoes*.

As noted earlier, young men and women were traditionally betrothed at birth. While young men were required to marry an older woman first, their later betrothal to a much younger wife would be initiated through a ceremony where her parents' approval of the marriage was confirmed. Once married, he would then be permitted to take further wives. Donald Thomson noted that one of the old men he worked with in Arnhem Land had acquired twenty-five wives during his life, although not all were alive when Thomson met him. Such marriages cemented the relationships between clans, as children were the members of their father's clan but also inherited resource rights in their mother's clan, which built their exchange networks across a much larger area. This genealogical and geographical investment was realised through marriage arrangements. In this respect, we see in *Ten Canoes* how the person most distant, both genealogically and geographically, is depicted not merely as a stranger but as a powerful sorcerer with the power to disrupt the lives of the main protagonists.

Traditionally, a special canoe that was shaped like a kayak with a pointed bow was used for traversing the reed-covered wetlands. This type of canoe had not been made within living memory and de Heer relied on the notes and illustrations made by Thomson to commission the vessels, which would be made by his Ganalbiŋu collaborators. That they were unfamiliar with the type of canoe that de Heer wanted was revealed during the film's preparation, as captured in the documentary film *Making Ten Canoes*.[13]

The age differential between a husband and wife is the second major theme of *Ten Canoes*. This is clearly one of the sources of tension that propels its plot and also the well-documented history of dispute, feuding and restitution institutions in Arnhem Land.

The American anthropologist Lloyd Warner arrived in Arnhem Land in the 1920s during a period of heightened tension. Feuding was taking many lives, and he documented the state of wife-raiding and warfare in his classic book, *A Black Civilization*.[14] The institutions of wife-raiding and the makarraṯa are well represented in *Ten Canoes*, with the armed makarraṯa ordeal initiated by the appearance of the sorcerer. According to de Heer's synopsis notes:

> One day, while the men are engaged in cutting each other's hair, a stranger approaches, without warning. The men are alarmed, especially when the Stranger claims he is there to trade in magic objects. The Stranger is given food and sent on his way by Ridjimiraril, although some of the other men want to kill him. The sorcerer comes to warn the men of the possible dangers, but declares the camp is safe. Life goes on as normal. Then Nowalingu, after a fight with Banalandju, vanishes. There's no trace of her. Ridjimiraril is convinced his beloved second wife was taken by

> that Stranger, but the consensus is that being jealous, she simply ran away. There's nothing Ridjimiraril can do. Months later an old uncle turns up for a visit and reports having seen Nowalingu in a distant camp with that stranger. The men are galvanised into action: a war party is prepared; it sets off, but without Yeeralparil. Both brothers cannot go ... if the older brother is killed, the younger brother must take over the other's wives. Yeeralparil hangs around the main camp in the hope of seeing Munandjarra, but Banalandju ensures a safe distance between the two. The war party returns, without Nowalingu: the old uncle's eyes must have deceived him. Ridjimiraril, still convinced it was the Stranger who took Nowalingu, slides into depression, until Birrinbirrin runs into camp with the news that the Stranger has been seen near the waterhole.[15]

The plot then rivals Shakespeare's characteristic twists and turns:

> Ridjimiraril tells Birrinbirrin he's going to talk to the Stranger but grabs his spears and takes off, Birrinbirrin puffing behind. Deep in the bush they see the Stranger, squatting [to defecate]. Ridjimiraril launches a spear. An inspection of the body, however, reveals that Ridjimiraril has killed the wrong stranger. There are sounds of approaching people. Ridjimiraril breaks the spear off and they quickly hide the body. But they did not hide that body well enough. Days later Ridjimiraril and Birrinbirrin are accosted by a group of warriors including the Stranger. They have identified

the spearhead in the Stranger's brother's body as having been made by Birrinbirrin, and they want payback. Ridjimiraril owns up, and the location and time for the payback ceremony is agreed to.

A sad little procession of men leave camp for the payback. This time Yeeralparil can go, as only one person is to be speared, either Ridjimiraril or his payback partner. Yeeralparil argues that it should be he, young and nimble, who ought partner his brother. Ridjimiraril agrees, and together the two brothers face the spears from the aggrieved Stranger's tribe. That is the law, and the law must be upheld.

Ridjimiraril is speared. Justice done, he is helped back to camp. Banalandju tends his wound, but instead of getting better, as he should, Ridjimiraril declines: it is as if a bad spirit has invaded his body. Even the sorcerer can do nothing. In his last moments before dying, Ridjimiraril staggers to his feet and begins to dance his own death dance ... then he collapses and dies.

After all the correct ceremony has been performed, Yeeralparil finally moves into the main camp, to be with his Munandjarra. But he's inherited a great deal more than he expected ...[16]

Yeeralparil has inherited the three jealous wives of his deceased brother, according to the custom of levirate marriage. He is aghast at his predicament, with each of the two older wives fighting for dominance in his affections and claiming their rights according to seniority. The hope of happiness with his beloved Munandjarra slips away as he realises his situation. In de Heer's notes, the present-day young man, Dayindi, is presented as much wiser:

Minygululu's story is over, the goose egg hunters return home. Dayindi has learnt his lesson, and when opportunity presents, he declines ... maybe someday he will have a wife, but it won't be someone else's.[17]

6

GENDERED BUSINESS

In desert Australia and neighbouring semi-arid regions, there is a demarcation between women's and men's spiritual life in relation to inner knowledge. Public life is less strict about this demarcation, although rules of respect and avoidance often apply. The ways that women shape the world in these Indigenous societies is different from the ways that men conduct their affairs, and this is often marked by special names, rituals and responsibilities.

To a very great extent, the world is gendered and dimorphous, though this is not to deny asymmetry and diversity in human and ancestral forms, gender and other attributes. The female and male attributes of most people, for instance, are also observed in landscapes, in special places and in most named things. How the constructs of femaleness and maleness are culturally shaped and defined is also diverse. There are many different understandings of gender and sexuality across regional traditions that are generally protected as being private in Indigenous legal systems and are therefore not generally discussed in public. Since colonisation, these traditional understandings have also been gradually overshadowed by competing Western attitudes and English-language definitions. Traditional definitions of sex, for example, are usually limited to purely procreative acts. However, on the Tiwi Islands, for example, there is very public support from local Indigenous elders for *yimpininni* or 'sister-girls': Tiwi trans women who hold full rights to perform traditional women's dances.[1] The original ancestors are sometimes considered to be asexual but also to switch species, change gender and change in number on their travels from homeland to homeland.

Some universals are nonetheless expected. Men and women often have their own martial arts traditions involving weapons. Women also give birth to children. This is not always the case, as some women do not give birth, but the notion of femaleness is associated with birthing, the great act of human creativity that informs so many cultural notions and practices.

WOMEN AND MEN

In northern and central Australia, where the Indigenous laws from precolonial times still operate and hold broad influence to a greater extent than elsewhere, women participate with men in many public ceremonial activities and have their own private rituals relating to birth, for instance. In these areas, they are key players in the conduct of affairs and ceremonies relating to homeland ownership. In the Yolŋu manikay (song) tradition, for example, the women's form of this style, known as *milkarri* or *ŋäthi* (crying), has the same lyrics and melodies as its male equivalent, and in some instances female leaders are renowned for knowing more song vocabulary than their male counterparts.

In desert societies, when women uphold laws, chief among their responsibilities are those associated with kinship, marriage and family. Many senior Aboriginal women have the power to hold together families as well as their language groups and communities. They have given birth to children and have grandchildren and, often, great-grandchildren. Their power derives from their roles as mothers and grandmothers and the interplay of marriage, family history, status, the size of their kinship networks and their assets, and their personal attributes.

Women who, in responsibility to their families, share food, essential goods, knowledge and a hospitable home where close kin are welcome to ensure that those closest to them thrive, and are more likely to be successful in binding their parents, children and others to their hearth or household. Those who do not share, are unkind, lazy or neglectful, speak ill of others or turn their kin away are unlikely to be successful in marriage and maintaining family ties.

Women elders have special roles in maintaining laws and guiding behaviour so that people follow the law. The status of 'elder' among women varies greatly across the Indigenous world, and there are many roles for such women. They have often mastered a suite of skills and learnt bodies of knowledge that might include traditional medicine and healing, midwifery, environmental knowledge, ancestral design, repertoires of song and dance, making tools and sacred objects and much more. Some are specialists in particular fields, and the women elders who are experts in these disciplines are sought after by their own immediate kin as well as others further afield. They are asked to be leaders of organisations and institutions, and influence political and policymaking outcomes with great success.

The Ngaanyatjarra, Pitjantjatjara and Yankunytjatjara (NPY) Women's Council is an example of a powerful women's body that governs a vast area across the Northern Territory, South Australia and Western Australia. Its directors are entirely women who are leaders in their own communities and recognised as 'law women': women who lead by asserting and holding their laws and customs in everyday life. They provide essential services across the region and have an unparalleled convening power that enables decisions to be made for it. Their annual general meetings draw together A<u>n</u>angu women from the NPY language groups and include women's ceremonies. Marcia Langton was honoured to be a patron of this council for a number of years, and at the end of her tenure a women's ceremony was held to acknowledge her service.

The work of the NPY Women's Council is especially important for the physical and emotional health of A<u>n</u>angu people. Health projects such as Munkaritja Kulinma/Kuliltjarra Nyinama (Stop and Think – Consider the Consequences), Nyakula Mukuringanyi Munu Arkani (If You Like What You See, Follow My Lead), and the Uti Kulintjaku (Words for Feelings) posters and fridge magnets provide insights into the council's leadership style, which encourages people towards responsible behaviours for themselves and for others. These resources are used by traditional *ngangkari* (healers) in A<u>n</u>angu communities and in workshops elsewhere to remedy physical and mental illnesses.[2] These healing practices are integral to A<u>n</u>angu ancestral law and fundamental to maintaining balance and harmony in A<u>n</u>angu communities.

To explain something of Indigenous women's beliefs, as much as can be permitted in the public domain, women who practise rituals and follow Indigenous laws usually have responsibilities of a sacred nature that are important to the life cycles of all human beings and particularly to women. Such events and states of being are marked and celebrated. They include:

- identifying the spirits that have induced pregnancy to name and affiliate the expected child
- the passage of young males and females from completion of puberty to reproductive adulthood, and the preparation of young people in a proper philosophical understanding of the sexual, reproductive and productive roles of men and women
- the emotional states that accompany the journey of life and the spiritual succour of ancestors who have experienced all states of being, including love, marriage, marital discord, adultery, and the inevitable consequences of sloth, greed, deception, vanity, murder and other antisocial behaviours

- the sacred meanings of local landscapes and their relevance to the peoples of those lands for the purposes of enabling procreation in other species
- the peculiarities of particular ecologies
- a range of matters of importance to social and economic life
- death as a journey and as a recycling of the essences of the environment as bequeathed by the ancestors.

Much of this knowledge is held and shared only by senior women. Such knowledge of women's business is held according to the precepts of Indigenous law, such that knowledge is gendered and life-giving. This knowledge is dangerous in the wrong hands and the most powerful of that knowledge, if shared inappropriately, may cause fatalities and other destructive consequences. It is held by appropriate elders and passed on to younger generations in a most careful way.

Women may become community leaders, healers, sorcerers or artists, as well as mothers and grandmothers who raise families. They may either come into special roles through inheritance, because their unique qualities are recognised when they are young, through reincarnation, or, of course, through training and practice under the tutelage of older, more knowledgeable women. They may become ritual leaders in the distinctive women's styles of ceremonial song and dance. Some of this is public but most of it is secret and available only to women of the family and other invited women.

SIGN LANGUAGE AND DANCE

Dancing brings country and ancestors to life, but singing country is vital. In daily life, singing is the act of calling the ancestral beings to action, and they, too, are often gendered. Exclusive women's societies keep these ancient traditions alive. For example, in the deserts and the Kimberley region, there are women's societies where widows live together and communicate by using a special sign language. Some take a vow of silence and use only sign language. British anthropologist Phyllis M Kaberry lived at the Forrest River Mission in the Kimberley region between 1935 and 1936, where she studied the lives of women. Her 1939 book *Aboriginal Woman: Sacred and Profane*[3] has been largely ignored by Australian anthropologists, but it is an extraordinary account of strong, independent women with their own rituals, beliefs and traditions that were the privilege of women.

One anthropologist who drew on Kaberry's work was Diane Bell, a feminist in an otherwise largely misogynistic discipline. In the 1980s, she lived in a women's society around Tennant Creek. In *Daughters of the Dreaming* (1983) she too describes women's religious life with its own distinctive laws, songs, rituals, sacred stories and sociality.[4] There is more in the literature, but such a paucity as to make us wonder why almost an entire continent of women's culture has been so assiduously disregarded.

We can see the distinctive culture of women's law or women's business in oratory, song, dance and design. Kokatha woman and choreographer Frances Rings brought an entire ancient landscape to life in her first full-length commission for Bangarra Dance Theatre in 2012. *Terrain* is a sublime, emotionally charged and dynamic rendition of Kati Thanda, a place of spiritual wonder in Arabana country in South Australia. The keeper of this country is the great spirit Warrena, whose extraordinary presence is felt throughout. Spread over more than a million square kilometres below sea level, this vast country, formerly called Lake Eyre, is the largest salt lake on the continent, with many smaller lakes and waterways. This fascinating landlocked lake ecosystem is renowned for its great transformations, cycling from dry to wet. When dry, it is a wonderland of crusted white glowing salt. On the rare occasions when big rains come or water flows from the wet monsoonal north down the dry rivers, the blinding white plains of salt that stretch to the horizon are deluged with water and become a gigantic lake with tendrils of connected waterways, hosting vast multitudes of birds and sudden, brief bursts of delicate flowers.

Rings' perception of Kati Thanda is manifested as nine sections or 'states of experiencing' the terrain and its physical and cultural features, its 'scars of millennia', the landscape-altering changes of floods and rain, and the sensuous connections between people and country are ever-present and powerful.[5] Rings lived in Kati Thanda and was guided by Arabana elder Reg Dodd to hear the sacred stories and sleep on his country to feel its power. To bring to life her journey across this land of lakes with its own weather system and seasons, she travelled with Dodd and other traditional owners, learning their culture and visiting ancestral women's and men's places to experience the stillness, silence, beauty and danger. She was fortunate to see it in its dry and very rare wet state, and in *Terrain* renders the femaleness and maleness of the landscape in her choreography of beautiful moving bodies.

Rings understood how difficult it is to express the nature of country, and yet she achieved something extraordinary in this dance work, showing the power of country and culture, creation stories, songlines, sacred sites and women's and men's laws that activate ancient connections between people and place.[6] *Terrain* gives us a lesson in how to learn about the web of life and its cycles through the gift of ancient laws. Being in country and learning about its specific stories from traditional owners is paramount. Above all, her perspective as a woman gives us a special insider understanding of how law and sacred culture bring country and its ancestral residents to life.

SINGING COUNTRY

Women who sing the country are precious. Their traditions are highly endangered. Filmmaker and television producer Rachel Perkins, whose ancestors are Arrernte and Kalkatungu, recognised this after her productions had securely established her as one of Australia's great artists. She grew up in Canberra, the daughter of the famous Charles Perkins, whose activist exploits and public service career wrought profound changes in White Australia's racist traditions. She longed to learn about her own culture in central Australia, and from the age of eighteen started the journey of studying its laws and traditions. She understood that 'song is key to unlocking the original Australian knowledge systems'.[7]

In 2015, Perkins established the Arrernte Women's Project to record women's songs that had been ignored by the hundreds of people who had studied central Australian cultures. These songs were facing extinction, so long after the colonisation of the region and the dominance of the White Australian system of regulating life through institutions such as schools and other governmental regimes. In her essay 'Songs to Live By', Perkins writes about the tragedy of the loss of these songs:

> [I]n the very last week of the camp, the ladies from the area with which my family is connected arrived. I had only just met these ladies, so could not be too familiar with them (which is a whole other story in itself). They spoke to each other in Arrernte, and the other women gathered around them. I could only understand a few words. What I did understand amid their conversation was the word 'dormitories'. My heart sank. They recounted that as girls they had been taken into the dormitories by the nuns. As a result, if there were songs, they hadn't learned them. I pretended to be doing some paperwork as I heard their conversation. It took everything in me to let that sad news pass by without remark.
>
> But that's how it unfolded: in the most mundane way. The songs were gone. The women left the camp soon after as there was nothing for them to do and not much to say. It was like when somebody dies. Nothing can be done but to miss them.[8]

Yet not all the songs were lost. Perkins's project started with a camp site: 'a cluster of newly made corrugated-iron rooms … in a bush location just outside Alice Springs ... and a recently prepared dance ground'.[9] She worked with the linguist and ethnomusicologist Myfany Turpin, as well as Arrernte women, including her sister Hetti and others in her family. Members of the Akeyulerre Healing Centre were especially keen to keep their traditions. Together they recorded and catalogued hundreds of songs, preserving a treasure of the world. About 100 Arrernte women visited the camp in its first month. Turpin had written: 'Traditional Aboriginal songs are regarded by Arrernte people ... as the quintessential repository of their law and culture.'[10] Her understanding of this fundament was later cited by Perkins: 'Knowing songs – including the dances, narratives and visual designs that accompany them – [is] a significant part of Aboriginal identity.'[11]

For Perkins, the challenge she undertook in attempting to preserve Arrernte women's songs meant delving into the depths of an ancient culture. 'Our continent was once alive with song,' she wrote.[12] This is how laws, knowledge and life-sustaining skills are carried and transmitted across hundreds of generations:

> In hundreds of languages, the Dreaming, which recounts how the world was created, was delivered in song. There were also environmental songs to bring forth abundant supplies of plants and animals. There were songs to heal the sick, songs to make a person fall in love, songs to turn boys into men, and songs just for entertainment.[13]

There are a few extraordinary exceptions to the long history of ignoring women. Before embarking on her recording, Perkins went to libraries and archives to find information and, she hoped, pre-existing recordings. She found *Songs of Central Australia* by the anthropologist TGH Strehlow. Perkins observed that this book detailing secret, sacred men's law is 'the most complete collection of cultural material of any First People in Australia and possibly the world'.[14] However, it contains nothing about women's law. Like Perkins, Barry Hill in his magnificent 2002 book *Broken Song* lamented this absence: 'No male white investigator has ever been able to get more than a faint hint of the women's mysteries in Central Australia ... we shall never know for certain the full extent of their vision.'[15] That was until Perkins, other Arrernte women and Turpin decided to do something about the existential threat to their song traditions.

In the AIATSIS archives in Canberra, Perkins found recordings of women singing, and these became the foundation of the Arrernte Women's Project. In the 1990s, the esteemed Arrernte elder MK Turner had worked with linguist Jenny Green, and Perkins copied the songs they had recorded 'onto 200 data sticks professionally [labeled with the designation]: *Arrelhe-kenhe* (Women's)'.[16]

Perkins' personal account of this work gives a rare glimpse into the world of women's law and its fragility:

> The Arrernte ladies have come to our camp to record what remains in their living memory of these songs. In line with a weekly schedule, they arrive in groups specific to their areas of land or 'estates' within the broader Arrernte territory. They

paint up their family members, erect the sacred symbols of their *Altyerre* [*Altyerrenge*] (Dreamings), and their ancient songs rise into the night sky with the embers from the fire. Everything is meticulously recorded by our all-female camera crew. The senior ladies carefully discuss who will guard these recordings into the future, to ensure that they are kept from reckless or inappropriate individuals. Taking the songs from the vault of their minds to an archive radically changes tradition. Yet they recognise it is crucial to do so, as the knowledge may well be lost if they don't. These women are our professors, and there are very few Arrernte women who still hold this knowledge.[17]

CEREMONIES AND LIFE CYCLES

Traditional ceremonies are great spectacles, and attendance is a prerequisite for advancement through the law for both men and women. Taking on ceremonial roles as one advances through law is an individual choice, but to do so means that such people acquire high status and responsibilities. Learning to perform ancestral song series is one such responsibility, as is ceremonial dancing. People begin to learn at a very young age.

Dancers are allowed a great deal of freedom of expression. They are barefoot and kick up the sand or soft earth they dance on. Their movements vary according to dance style. In some styles, they keep their feet close to the ground to symbolise their connection with the earth or emotional states. Other movements and gestures communicate specific ancestral beings and emotions. Pounding the earth in unison, leaping into the air and imitations of particular animals are some of the movements to be seen.[18] Dancers also call out in response to singers and musicians. This is often to express the connections of ancestral species and events to significant places.

Male dancers across different regions often adorn themselves with ochre paints, colourful cloth wrapped around their bodies, feathered headdresses, gumleaf anklets and other decorations to indicate their various affiliations. Women wear swaying skirts and, when dancing topless, also paint their bodies with ochre. Body and face painting is a spectacular feature of Aboriginal dances at ceremonies. Each design painted on the skin has a specific meaning. They all tell stories about country and ancestral beings. Related designs are also applied to ceremonial objects and everyday items.[19]

In northern and central Australia, ceremonial songs are generally sung in long series. Each song is short but is typically repeated. There are also unique songs and fun songs for entertainment. Women sing in a variety of styles. For example, following a death, women will lead keening or crying songs. In central desert communities, groups of women sing sacred song cycles while others clap with cupped hands to keep the beat.

Women's law requires that certain rituals are performed concerning the dangerous and nourishing powers of sexual attraction, courting, marriage and related emotional states. These empower women to control these states and explain their significance to younger women. Another responsibility of law women is to keep and practice medicinal and healing knowledge. These are applied to benefit individuals and groups via ritual acts for healing and sometimes marriage. Certain sacred sites are associated with this knowledge and power.

In many Indigenous societies, women are fighters. Some have martial arts styles that they learn for defensive, offensive and punitive purposes. The special knowledge of senior law women includes a range of practical and spiritual practices for when conflict arises, and they may take vengeance on others through fighting or sorcery when they feel aggrieved.

Law women also have specific roles in mourning and mortuary rituals, including funerary rites, coronial inquisitions to determine cause of death, and exacting punishments. Funeral ceremonies are often celebrations of the ancestral connections of the deceased; but they are now often mixed with Christian traditions and sometimes incorporate other cultural influences as well.

GENDER AND RITUAL

Women's ritual observances and ceremonies, including songs and keening, are not only vehicles for ancestral accounts but also performative devices for emphasising important states, emotions and events that give expression to a wide range of life's concerns.

Celebrations of ancestral journeys are convened, involving songs, dances, ritual objects and body painting, to call upon ancestors by re-enacting their sacred encounters. Places are imbued with ancestral spirits, and spirits are gendered. The gender of the ancestors is one of the essential attributes of their unceasing existence. There are places where only women may go, and places where only men may go.

The relationship of places to births, and the birthing rites that have taken place at them, are remembered in many Indigenous cultures in Australia by the trees that grow there. These are known as 'birthing trees', and it is said that they hold some spiritual essence of the people born under them. Other sacred places along riverbanks, apart from these birthing places, require gender-specific observances to acknowledge their intrinsic ancestral meanings and essences.

Ceremonies include roles that women perform in public. These include public sequences of male initiation ceremonies and rituals for observing important species, particularly plants, to encourage their reproduction. The ancestors and places associated with these species are celebrated in these rituals.

Senior women, especially midwives and healers, often have extensive knowledge concerning the care of women and their babies, birthing rituals and practices, rituals for investing the spiritual essence and power of particular births into places and trees, and rituals for activating certain powers in newborn infants.

Gendered places have been discussed by the anthropologist Deborah Bird Rose in her Australian Heritage Council report *Nourishing Terrains*:

> Dreamings travelled; they were sometimes in human form, and sometimes in animal or other form. But whatever the form, they were almost inevitably either male or female. Dreaming men and women sometimes walked separately and thus created gendered places. There are now women's places and men's places; places which are associated with one or the other because Dreaming

> made it that way. There are varying degrees of exclusion: places where men can go but must be quiet, places where they can look but not stare, where they can walk but not camp, and then there are places where men cannot go at all, ever. There are places where men cannot drink the water, cannot even look at the smoke that rises from women's country. And of course the same is also true with respect to men's places, men's country.[20]

The gendering of landscape and social organisation is typical of Indigenous life. Women make strategic decisions that form part of a repertoire of strategies for sustaining land-holding group identity and continuity.

PLACES, ART, DREAMS, SELF

The status of the Indigenous master painters is key to understanding people's fascination with their artistic outputs. They endured the frontier and retained a magnificent vision of their homelands that has transferred to their art works. The endurance of their homelands as represented in art is an especially vivid means for those who wish to throw off the yoke of frontier culture to engage with Indigenous visions of landscape.

In the late 20th century, art critics singled out Emily Kame Kngwarreye for special attention. In most respects, the painterly style of Kngwarreye distinguishes her work from that of others. Part of this attraction to her work arguably lies in the fact of her female gender and the shock to curators and critics in the male-dominated Indigenous art market that a woman could be of high status and represent dreamings in her work. Kngwarreye's command of painting the dreamings of her landscape was shocking to the tired old critics of Indigenous art. Why should this be after everything that women anthropologists have written for the past two decades? It is because seeing is believing. These critics had not seen ground paintings and sand sculptures in use at women's ceremonies because they are secret and sacred. There had been a national suspicion that there was no women's law at all, and this was bolstered by vicious attacks in the 1990s on Ngarrindjeri women who sought to protect their sacred sites on Hindmarsh Island in South Australia.[21]

Like other Indigenous master painters, the age and status of Kngwarreye before her passing in 1996 meant that she already had one foot in the dreaming. Her extreme age and apparent seniority as a law woman were key to the infatuation of critics and audiences with her work. She came from a small central desert culture and lived according to ancient traditions. Her primary audience was urban, coastal and hyper-consumerist, while she lived in the remote desert, in austere and ascetic conditions.

For Kngwarreye, her task as a law woman was to uphold her Anmatyerre dreamings for future generations. She often travelled for traditional hunting and gathering along the Sandover River, on lands that were confiscated and granted to White settlers as pastoral leases from the 1860s. She was already advanced in years when those lands were returned to Anmatyerre people under the *Aboriginal Land Rights (NT) Act 1976*.

The iconography of male master painters usually concerns the sacred elements of large regional landscapes and water sources, and ancestral species and their creative deeds. Women however, being gatherers of vegetable foods and small mammals, instead tend to paint plant species rather than large species such as wallaby and emu. This is a main source of gender differentiation in Indigenous art and explains much about Kngwarreye's style. Whereas settler Australians saw an empty wilderness, Indigenous people saw a busy spiritual landscape filled with ancestors and evidence of their creative feats.[22] Drawing on the deep well of law that she upheld, Kngwarreye produced a grand vision, wrongly interpreted by critics as abstract in nature, of the spiritual and natural forces she saw in the world around her.

POWER AND RIGHTS

The most important criterion for exercising power is traditional land ownership. Women are landowners too. But their rights in land and how they are transmitted have been largely ignored by the professionals who make a living from Indigenous dispossession. How women hold together their families and wider kinship networks is a source of their power.

Exercising authority over territory and its governance is never straightforward, and in small-scale societies the influence of an individual can be great if she is politically skilled. The skills involved in governing territory and resource use – such as oratory, hospitality, ritual exchange and marriage betrothals – might enhance a woman's claim to rights and responsibilities.

Women play a key part in maintaining land tenure systems and the succession of land ownership. Indigenous land tenure systems and succession processes are dynamic and flexible. Having largely survived colonisation and attempts at White assimilation, they provide important opportunities in a range of social affairs. Many, but not all, anthropologists have generated myths depicting these laws as the domain of men alone, with all ancestry reckoned through male lineages. In far too many cases, Indigenous people have had to deal with anthropologists who absolutely deny the role of women in maintaining Indigenous laws relating to land ownership.

Anthropologists working in Australia have debated the nature of Indigenous land tenure for decades, persisting with a dogmatic account of male-oriented systems that largely exclude women from land ownership and related affairs. The few exceptions in this are mainly women. When Aboriginal land rights in the Northern Territory and native title rights were recognised by the Australian Government in 1976 and 1994 respectively, White male anthropologists enshrined this dogma in legislation and practice.[23] Despite this, judges who heard ensuing land rights and native title cases were able to recognise the role of women in land ownership. Indeed, a very slow shift occurred as judges themselves pointedly remarked on the importance of women in land rights.

The anthropological theory of patrilineal rights in land tenure originated in a 1971 land rights case heard in the Supreme Court of the Northern Territory over a major bauxite mining operation on Yolŋu homelands. The judge's ruling in this case, *Milirrupum v Nabalco*,[24] was a heavy blow to Yolŋu people, whose ancient rights were deemed to be not legally recognisable by the Australian Govermnent. This case and the commission of inquiry that followed fascinated anthropologists of the time.[25] The Yolŋu system thus became the template for the way anthropologists would explain all Indigenous land tenure to courts. Yet even the Yolŋu system, which was fetishised by anthropologists, recognises extensive land tenure laws that pass through female lineages, usually within reŋgitj alliances (see Chapter 4).

For Indigenous groups who have endured rapid population loss as a result of frontier violence and disease, forced removals and other impacts of colonisation, maternal relatives take on a special role in succession arrangements to homelands where the original ownership group has not survived. Understanding the role of grandmothers in both ownership and ritual arrangements through female lineages is vital in a wide range of contexts. They and their brothers are important in succession processes.

In land rights and native title claims, some judges have agreed with Indigenous women claimants, though women witnesses have often been silenced by the organisation and conduct of claims. Therefore, the significance of women's law in the general affairs of society has largely been missed in these cross-cultural legal contexts. But when women law-holders have been given appropriate opportunities to speak, they have often explained the importance of their life-enhancing ceremonies and expanded our understanding of Indigenous property laws.

The anthropologist Catherine Berndt, who observed women's ceremonies in the Kimberley region, reported that a woman passed on rights in homeland from her father to her daughter because of the absence of any male heirs in their group.[26] Women's ceremonies alone were enough to secure the status of women as holders of these rights.

The rights of women as members of ownership groups alongside male heirs has come to be readily acknowledged in anthropological and legal literature. Women are also members of related groups with ceremonial responsibilities for managing and scrutinising landowner affairs, thereby ensuring fidelity to traditions. These relatives and their roles are called djuŋgayi, for example, by Yolŋu people (see Chapter 4) and *kurtungurlu* by Warlpiri people. Anthropologist Nicolas Peterson has noted that female lineages can be a key factor in succession processes via different matrilineally traced ties to related groups among siblings from a common father.[27]

Maternal relationships are not an unusual feature of Indigenous ownership systems but, rather, like male relationships, provide continuity through time for all related ownership groups. Ceremonies and religious concerns focused on maternal relationships further bind together relatives and their various homelands to provide a wide range of regional choices and opportunities.

Women negotiate homeland and marriage affairs actively in many succession cases, legitimately pursuing their interests and those of their descendants. Their interests in prospective grandchildren and how those grandchildren acquire homeland affiliations are among their key concerns. Grandmothers are a powerful influence upon all interested parties here. Indigenous people readily acknowledge that the approval of grandmothers for politicking in affairs of this kind is crucial to successful outcomes. We must therefore be careful to better understand women's rights in homelands and the ways that women's law is reflected in gendered landscapes.

7

WISDOM AND LEADERSHIP

> *Nyampurla kuja karlipa nyinami, Wawirri-kirlangurla ngurrara-rla, maannginyanyirlipa Wanya-parnta-wiyi, yugunganpa pinarri-mani paarr-pardinjaku, Warlawurru-piya, kankarlarra pura, nguruwana* 'To live in the homeland of the Kangaroo, first understand the Emu, who will teach us to soar high like the Wedge-tailed Eagle.'
>
> Warlpiri proverb as told by Wanta Pawu[1]

There is one final detail in Michael Jakamara Nelson's *Possum and Wallaby Dreaming* design of 1985 that is key to understanding how Indigenous systems of law in Australia traditionally function. As discussed in Chapter 4, before the gradual expansion of schools and universities across the continent in the 20th century, Indigenous ceremonies provided the only known systems of formal education in Australia. Ceremonial processes induct people into law. They teach and contextualise appropriate behaviours and values that people should aspire to emulate in their daily life, and repeated ceremonial participation encourages people to grow in wisdom throughout their lives. People who demonstrate good judgement and the potential to hold positions of responsibility are progressed through the formal educational pathways that ceremonies provide.

We noted in Chapter 3 that *Possum and Wallaby Dreaming* shows twelve animal tracks, with each animal respectfully walking on all fours from the four cardinal directions towards the Jardiwarnpa ceremony depicted at the design's centre. Three possums travel from the north, three wallabies travel from the east, three possums travel from the south, and three wallabies travel from the west. This total number of twelve animal tracks is not arbitrary, nor is their grouping into four alternating sets of three animals of each species. This is a very deliberate representation of the way that Warlpiri people can progress through a traditional annual cycle of four main ceremonies that structure the Warlpiri education system under ancestral law.

Participants in these main ceremonies can come from all four of the Warlpiri patri-semimoieties. However, the leadership and delivery of the ceremonies is distributed evenly across each of them. People progress through the traditional male and female forms of these ceremonies through a series of twelve sequential grades that are evenly distributed across four main ceremonies. Completing an entire sequence of all twelve grades therefore involves doing all four ceremonies thrice.

In Wanta's own family tradition, children are introduced to ceremonial life through the public context of the Jardiwarnpa, which they must attend three times to complete grades 1–3. Males, for example, are then initiated into young adult responsibilities at puberty through grades 4–6 in the seclusion of the Kurdiji ceremony.

More advanced learning is undertaken through grades 7–9, in the seclusion of the Kankarlu ceremony. The three final grades, which reinforce previous learnings in the secluded Kurdiji ceremony, are designed to train *yuwarlpiri* (people-keepers) – fully knowledgeable and authorised Warlpiri leaders.

Grades 1–9 are named after progressively bigger and more powerful birds of prey, who hunt in their own ascending layers of airspace over the Warlpiri homelands. Grade 1 is named after the small *Karr-karnpa* (Brown Goshawk), who flies through the underbrush to flush out small prey. *Winy-winpya* (Spotted Harrier) followed by *Warukuparluku-parluku* (Nankeen Kestrel) complete the first three Jardiwarnpa grades. The ensuing Kurdiji grades are *Purrkura* (Whistling Kite), *Kalantirri* (Black-breasted Buzzard) and *Yaalakapara* (Peregrine Falcon), while the Kankarlu grades that follow are *Kirrkalanji* (Brown Falcon), *Purla-purla* (Black Kite) and *Warlawurru* (Wedge-tailed Eagle). The names of the final three senior leadership grades are withheld from public discourse.[2]

Walking inwards from the edges of *Possum and Wallaby Dreaming* towards its central Jardiwarnpa ceremony, the twelve animals represented traverse the vast distances of their various homelands. However, reading their tracks around the central Jardiwarnpa fire motif like a clock, their combined journeys also traverse time and the lifelong pursuit of wisdom through participating in ceremonial law.

LEARNING TO FLY

The soaring wedge-tailed eagle can hunt from as far as 2 kilometres above the Earth's surface, and its power and prowess is greatly venerated in Warlpiri law. When all the birds gathered to learn how to fly at Yinapaka (Lake Surprise), they turned to Wedge-tailed Eagle as their greatest hunter and asked him to teach them. Wedge-tailed Eagle replied that he could not teach them, when Emu suddenly appeared at the meeting uninvited. Upon learning of their request, Emu offered to teach the other birds himself. But because Emu is a flightless bird, his help was roundly ridiculed and refused, and so he left to continue his journey. The other birds then turned back to Wedge-tailed Eagle and begged him to teach them. But Wedge-tailed Eagle held firm, explaining that he could not teach them, because he had not taught himself how to fly. Emu was his teacher and they had just him chased away. To this day, Wedge-tailed Eagle resents all the other birds and will prevent them from entering his exclusive airspace high above the Earth. His downward view of the landscape from above, which informs the way that the most senior Warlpiri leaders paint designs, is the most comprehensive, but he still respects the superior knowledge of Emu.

This lesson casts Emu as the ultimate teacher – an astute and wise old man, whose knowledge of flight and ability to teach the Wedge-tailed Eagle, the greatest of all hunters, are obscured by his flightless appearance. When children are introduced to the idea of attending their first Jardiwarnpa ceremony, their preliminary ceremonial rank is *Yakalpa* (Emu Chick) and elders will typically ask them: 'Who has ever seen an emu fly?' The answer to this riddle, like all such cryptic learnings in ceremonial law, is hidden in the natural environment.

The term *Pirli-mangkuru* can be translated as 'Sea of Stones' and is the Warlpiri name for the Milky Way. This vast sea of stars in the black void of space is thought to be the eternal home of Warlpiri ancestors; the floor of another world where the stars are campfires lit by the old people every night. But on the night of a new moon in the Tanami Desert, far away from city lights, the Milky Way can also be seen to harbour other, darker constellations.

Mostly comprising dark nebulae that can only be seen clearly during a new moon, the Flying Emu constellation answers that traditional riddle: 'Who has ever seen an emu fly?' It hides in plain view for all who are experienced and wise enough to see it. The Coalsack dark nebula is the Flying Emu's head. It adjoins the Southern Cross, which he wears as a crown just like the single white feather that Warlpiri people wear as a ceremonial headdress. Opposite the Southern Cross, the Coalsack joins a thin neck of dark nebulae that stretches through the Pointers, which are a woman's ceremonial digging stick caught in the Flying Emu's throat. His dark-nebulae torso extends down through Scorpius, and the bright-yellow nebulae that line his stomach are the fire of the Jardiwarnpa ceremony in his belly. His dark-nebulae legs then stretch backwards behind his tail.

The Flying Emu constellation wheels through the sky every year, and its position marks the four Warlpiri seasons. In the Jardiwarnpa song series led by the Wanya-parnta patri-semimoiety, the four seasons are indicated by the stations of the Flying Emu overhead. The series opens with items that establish the Flying Emu in his eternal and immutable ancestral state in the Milky Way, before subsequent song items introduce the four seasons in turn. The wet season, associated with the Wanya-parnta, is when the Flying Emu is dormant and sleeps beneath the sea. The cool season, associated with the Parra, is when the Flying Emu wakes, shakes the water off his feathers, and launches himself out of the water. The dry season, associated with the Wawirri, is when the Flying Emu finds himself in full flight (see Figure 10), astonished to see that both of his legs are stretched out backwards in the sky behind him. Finally, the hot season, associated with the Munga, is when the Flying Emu loses altitude and dives back into the water to sleep again. It is towards the

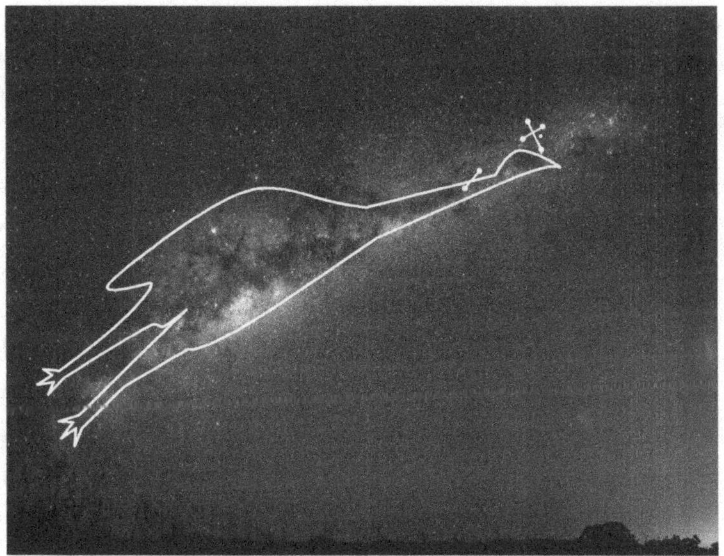

FIGURE 10: The Warlpiri Flying Emu constellation with the Emu in full flight, both of his legs stretched out behind him in the sky.

end of the hot season – usually in October, when the digging-stick Pointers touch the horizon and the Southern Cross becomes a great yarla (yam) buried beneath Earth's curvature – that the Jardiwarnpa ceremony commences and the Flying Emu's passage through the night sky begins again.

Looking down upon the Earth from his vantage in the night sky, the two constellations adjacent to the Flying Emu's crown (the Southern Cross) explain the Left and Right matrimoieties (see Chapter 3). To the right of the Southern Cross are the digging-stick Pointers, and to the left are two Magellanic clouds that form the entry and exit holes of a goanna nest. Their names refer to the great wisdom and arduous challenges that people will typically encounter when advancing through the ceremonial grades of learning. As in many such systems of learning and accreditation around the world, earlier grades are easy but grow progressively harder as you advance through them.

Associating the digging-stick Pointers as they touch the horizon with the name Karnanganja (I am going to eat and drink) casts ceremonies as a direct conduit for accessing the law of the Southern Cross. When buried as a great yarla beneath the Earth's curvature in the hot season, the Southern Cross represents the nourishing feast of ancestral knowledge to be had through ceremonial participation. The association of the two Magellanic clouds as goanna holes with the name Yankirri (people coming and going), however, acknowledges that ceremonial participation inevitably becomes increasingly difficult as you advance through the grades and are required to develop greater resilience and command over your emotions and actions. There is therefore no expectation that all people will necessarily complete all grades, or even be capable of doing so, without sometimes taking long breaks in between. The entry and exit holes of the goanna nest therefore represent the free choice of individuals to progress through ceremonial grades at their own pace and only as far as they want. Advancement though the ceremonial grades can also be withheld from people who have breached the law. To gain re-entry, males, for example, must discover for themselves how to pluck a breast feather from a deadly wedge-tailed eagle for presentation to his ceremonial leaders.

Overall, then, the Flying Emu is the ultimate teacher and a paragon of ceremonial learning and knowledge to which all should aspire. He takes uninitiated Emu Chicks and, through graded learning in ceremonies, equips them for life in the land of the Red Kangaroo by teaching them how to soar high like Wedge-tailed Eagle. His teachings link earth to sky so that as people ascend through the ceremonial grades they can grow through the wisdom of ancestors, who dwell eternal in the Milky Way. Ultimately, the Flying Emu exemplifies all the qualities of executive wisdom and good judgement that are highly desirable in fully trained and accredited Warlpiri leaders who have devoted their lives to completing and, in turn, teaching all grades of ceremonial law.

EXECUTIVE WISDOM

Ceremonial leaders hold and practise a kind of executive wisdom that simultaneously models and regulates preferred attitudes and behaviours across society. They exemplify and moderate the respectfulness, good judgement and responsible behaviours encouraged in people, and are expected to do this with great intelligence, tact and patience.

Ultimately, ceremonial leaders are required to become experienced teachers because they are chiefly responsible for training all potential successors who can ultimately replace them in carrying on their group's traditions. Their generosity of time and spirit when teaching good students is typically boundless, and they are highly attuned to identifying talented and willing protégés, both within and outside their immediate families, who hold aptitude and the capacity for long-term commitment in carrying on their group's traditions.

While interest, aptitude and birth order within families can influence advancement through ceremonial grades, these factors alone do not guarantee eventual admission to being a fully qualified leader. The pathway to leadership is long, arduous and costly in terms of personal investment. Likelihood of success is limited and ultimately linked to a student's willingness to learn, to inconvenience themselves for the pursuit of greater learning and to trust in their leaders when facing challenging learning experiences.

Formal ceremonial educational systems require prospective leaders to master the enormous lifelong endeavour of learning, executing and directing all legal processes and the variable parts of all corresponding song, dance and design content that are necessary to run complex ceremonies for any potential purpose. Ceremonial songs and the language and knowledge that they carry contribute a critically important facet of this leadership training. The language carried in ceremonial songs typically extends beyond everyday vocabularies and preserves old words and sophisticated terms found nowhere else. Leaders use these extended vocabularies of specialised song language when speaking formally to educate protégés, mount arguments, mediate disputes and negotiate fair outcomes in ways that demonstrate their wisdom and vastly outclass less experienced parties. Ceremonial leaders are therefore renowned for their formidable formal public-speaking skills and are typically able to speak about important and challenging topics in sensitive yet compelling ways.

As well as this vast knowledge and influence, prospective leaders are required to develop great resilience to adversity and control their emotions and responses, so they can engage in diplomacy and mediate difficult situations respectfully and effectively. Leaders who fail at this may well remain leaders in name but typically will not be widely trusted, respected or invited by other leaders to collaborate in running combined ceremonies or engage in diplomatic exchanges. Because legal authority and ceremonial responsibilities are distributed so evenly across different related groups in Indigenous societies, leaders must typically be able to engage in respectful and productive relationships with other leaders and their charges to achieve desired outcomes.

Beyond these core responsibilities, leaders may also hold expertise in a variety of different specialisations. Among the kinds of specialisations traditionally practised are arbitrating the process of conveying ownership in a homeland between different groups, healing and administering traditional medicines to the sick, birthing and midwifery, training warriors in combat and espionage, planning travels between homelands to align with ceremonial commitments and seasonal harvesting opportunities, and plotting long journeys between vast regions over land and sea by navigating the night sky and deep currents.

Because respect and humility are so highly valued and encouraged as desirable traits in Indigenous societies, ceremonial leaders often act in everyday public settings with a gentleness and grace that renders them almost imperceptible to outsiders. They will often sit back in silence and act through highly capable protégés of lesser ceremonial authority, such as their older children, while remaining fully engaged in important matters and wielding ultimate legal authority in formal decision-making.

Leaders will often say, however, that no one can ever truly hold ultimate authority: firstly, because ceremonial responsibilities are ideally evenly distributed across different related groups in Indigenous societies; and secondly, because all authority ultimately flows from the original ancestors. Even the oldest and most experienced of leaders will acknowledge that nature itself, which remains richly encoded with ancestral knowledge in its myriad forms and cycles, is the ultimate teacher and can always show new ways of understanding reality and our evolving circumstances.

Once they have mastered their own system of law and governance, leaders may seek to establish diplomatic exchanges into other regions to attain knowledge and seniority through the parallel systems of ceremonial law practised there. These kinds of leaders never cease their own betterment and networking through ceremonial learning, and usually become the most respected of all.

Today, this reverence for the pursuit of personal betterment through lifelong learning extends to all kinds of educational pursuits, including those that culminate in vocational and university qualifications. It is no coincidence, for example, that the term *mim'pu* in the Yolŋu languages – which refers to the raised scars traditionally earnt for completing ceremonial grades – is now also used to denote newer forms of educational attainment, including graduating from high school, a vocational course or a university degree.

Arbitrating matters that can provoke legal challenges, such as conveying a homeland's ownership from one group to another, can be very risky and potentially harmful to the leaders involved. As such, they typically undertake such work in ways that mask their identities from everyone except the other leaders directly concerned. The restriction and secrecy provisions that surround the highest ceremonial levels of Indigenous law and governance structures therefore serve two key purposes: they ensure that entrants to each successive ceremonial grade are not deprived of the benefits of these vital learning experiences by having them spoiled in advance; and they limit the direct exposure of leaders to unfiltered public expectations and demands so that they are not overwhelmed and exhausted by the heavy demands and challenges of leadership.

In Yolŋu society, for example, it is d̲ilak (elders) who hold ultimate responsibility and authority for making binding legal decisions. They are also responsible for training and appointing qualified ceremonial leaders beneath them who are l̲iya-ŋärra'mirri (wise) and can direct complex public ceremonies in their entirety. As we discussed in Chapter 3, the terms d̲alkarramirri and djirrikaymirr are specifically applied to mature men of Yirritja and Dhuwa clans respectively who are trained to lead public ceremonies and authorised to sing likan yäku (joining name) invocations on behalf of their clans. The root words *dalkarra* and *djirrikay* refer to the respective Yirritja and Dhuwa ancestral powers vested as legal authority in these public ceremonial leaders.

Becoming dalkarramirri or djirrikaymirr is, of course, a long and arduous process entailing many years of diligent study and practice, and the accumulation of märr (enlightenment) through good deeds and ceremonial devotion (see Chapter 4). Their training entails mastery of performing all song, dance and design parts for all of their clan's manikay series and knowing how to combine these in public ceremonies with likan yäku singing to activate ancestral relationships with corresponding homelands. They must also learn how to train and direct large groups of performers and artisans when preparing and delivering complex public ceremonies across a broad array of novel contexts.[3]

Dalkarramirri and djirrikaymirr leaders are charged with the vital tasks of faithfully maintaining the expansive bodies of ancestral knowledge about their homelands that their manikay series carry, while simultaneously growing and extending this tradition to accommodate reinterpretations of old understandings and responses to new information and circumstances. They constantly rearrange and reinterpret the established themes and meanings of their manikay in response to arising circumstances of celebration, loss, negotiation and commemoration, and have long used the manikay tradition to record and regulate significant intercultural influences, such as the extensive history of Yolŋu trade with South-East Asian seafarers. In these ways, each generation of ḏalkarramirri and djirrikaymirr leaders contributes their own wisdom to the greater body of ancestral knowledge, like each new layer of ash deposited upon an old campfire site.[4]

Indigenous healers work to maintain the wellbeing of their communities by applying a range of learnt traditional methods. They train under experienced healers, often from a young age, and learn Indigenous ways of understanding human physiology and psychology. The causes of disease are understood in terms of ancient cultural knowledge that has served thousands of generations well. While women and men may become healers, the role of women is vital to the health and wellbeing of women and children, and often men as well. Such healers are known as *marrŋgitj* in the Yolŋu languages of north-east Arnhem Land and ngangkari in the Aṉangu languages.[5] Healers have collaborated with Western medical professionals and scientists and, today, are welcome in clinics and hospitals where their traditions are held to be important. The Indigenous values that healers affirm, such as ideals of harmony and balance, can instil confidence in Indigenous patients, especially when they are afraid and resistant to Western health care.

The role of healers is to maintain harmony and balance in the people they treat and across society as a whole. Their complex cultural principles and methods involve the interconnection of people and country with the ancestral world and the perceivable physical world. They also involve the influences of ancestral beings upon the world. Healers may advise their patients to use Western medical treatments, but in communities where Western health care is absent or limited, their treatments for fever, infections, wounds, diarrhoea, mental distress and other common ailments are frequently sought out and used. When patients are overcome with the belief that they will die, healers bring them back to a state of engagement with life. They improve marital relationships by encouraging harmony, and can even enable people to marry by spiritually influencing their states of being.

Herbal treatments are also used, along with the application of heat and massage. Indigenous knowledge of medicinal substances in plants and trees depends on an intimate understanding of local environments, vegetation, climate and geography, along with learnt traditional knowledge about the medicinal use of plants.[6] Despite colonial dispossession, much of this traditional knowledge survives and is practised across vast areas of Australia. The impact of colonisation on Australia's important vegetation communities has caused hunger and sickness, but the persistence of these traditions gives hope, because people want harmony and balance in their lives.

NEGOTIATING CHANGE

Today, the outward appearances and backgrounds of Indigenous people from different parts of Australia offer no indication of their potential involvement in ceremonial law or where ceremonial leaders and participants can be found. Participants regularly travel vast distances to ceremonies, and this has only increased with the expansion of road and air travel options within the past century.

Because ceremonial law is grounded in values of balance, respect, responsibility and betterment over entirely alien Western notions of race and rivalry, people who are not Indigenous Australians have also been included in ceremonies for as long as they have been in Australia. As a rule, however, guest admission is by invitation only. Even then, it is relatively rare and is slow to manifest over many years of shared trust and experiences. It is also important to know that appearing at any ceremony unknown and uninvited will be sure to cause offence, as will requests to be invited.

Guests who are unfamiliar with ceremonial processes will often experience great confusion over which ones are public, partly because this can vary greatly in different regions of Australia. Generally, it is highly unlikely that any guest would be invited to attend a ceremony that is not public. If you were at a ceremony where men, women and children were all in attendance, it would most likely be a public one. Even so, it is always respectful and necessary to ask elders present whether your stories and records of any ceremony can be shared with others afterwards.

While the undue pressures of colonisation and assimilationist policies sent some systems of ceremonial law into dormancy, particularly in the most populated parts of Australia during the 20th century, there have been significant sustained attempts within the past quarter-century to revitalise ceremonial law in regions where continuous practice had inadvertently broken down. This does not, however, remedy the present-day endangerment of ceremonial traditions that remain in continuous practice despite the enduring disadvantage and the external pressures of contemporary life.

Some ceremonial leaders have become increasingly vocal about this issue. Upon being appointed as a Professorial Fellow of the Indigenous Knowledge Institute at the University of Melbourne, the Warlpiri leader Wanta Pawu remarked:

> All these stories, all this knowledge: I'm trying to share these as much as I can with anyone who will listen … People need to know. It's time for me to get it, to put this knowledge out there. Things are getting desperate now. There are only a few of us who still hold this knowledge. We want to share to Warlpiri and, more widely, to those who will listen. I'm looking forward to all the different things we are going to do.[7]

The Milpirri Festival – founded in collaboration with Darwin's Tracks Dance Company in 2005 – was Wanta's response as a Warlpiri leader to the first youth suicide in his hometown, Lajamanu.[8] Despite the centrality of ceremonial law and learning to the Warlpiri way of life before the 21st century, an entire generation of young Warlpiri people has been raised at Lajamanu with no access to regular annual ceremonies, reduced understanding of the formal Warlpiri language needed to learn traditional songs and no clear understanding of Warlpiri social organisation. As Wanta has explained above, all these interwoven systems are now on the verge of lapsing completely. The Lajamanu community has largely attributed the cause of that first youth suicide to the directionlessness that this erosion of the Warlpiri social order has instilled in their young people:

> There was a suicide at Lajamanu, maybe two years earlier before the ... [first] Milpirri event. For that loss for that youngfella [young person], it was like having the guts taken out of the Warlpiri nation. How do we find a way to teach ourselves again, and to remind ourselves that each one of us is precious?[9]

The Milpirri Festival envisions a new future for Warlpiri society in which traditional knowledge and values can continue to exist and be practised in the contemporary world, and be understood to hold important lessons about balance, respect, responsibility and achievement for people all over the world. At the festival's core lies Wanta's own guiding philosophy of ngurra-kurlu (home-having), which builds upon the natural template of the Southern Cross to identify five Warlpiri principles that are crucial to maintaining your sense of self and direction in life.[10] As discussed in Chapter 3, these are jaru (language), warlalja (kin), kuruwarru (law), manyuwana (ceremony) and walya (land).

The Milpirri Festival is just one of many examples of leaders resourcefully drawing on their knowledge of ceremonial law in response to changing circumstances and new challenges. Indigenous systems of law have always been highly adaptable and long enabled people in Australia to survive world-changing events, both societal and environmental. It is this adaptability that allowed people in Australia to endure both the last Ice Age peak around 20,000 years ago and the last major sea-level rise some 10,000 years ago. Yolŋu people of north-east Arnhem Land, for example, still perform traditional manikay about freshwater vents on the sea floor that were sacred springs above ground millennia ago, and inland lakes like the one at Gapuwiyak that were once ceremony grounds.[11]

Within the past millenium, Indigenous groups living along the Kimberley and Arnhem Land coastlines of northern Australia had developed beneficial international trading relationships with seafarers from South-East Asia. The earliest archaeological evidence of this contact is a pottery shard found on Groote Eylandt in Arnhem Land that has been radiocarbon-dated to the 12th century.[12] Warlpiri people in the Tanami Desert clearly knew of this foreign contact as they traditionally walked the ancient Emu trade route to the Kimberley coastline. Their Jardiwarnpa ceremonies still sing of how the Flying Emu swims from the Kimberley coastline across the world's oceans to other continents and islands in the Southern Hemisphere at the change between each of the four seasons. This indicates that knowledge of the world beyond Australia has long been embedded in Warlpiri law, which embraces a global perspective that can hold meaning for all.

By the 1750s, large commercial boat fleets were making annual voyages to northern Australia from the port city of Makassar in the Sultanate of Gowa on the Indonesian island of Sulawesi. By the first half of the 19th century, some thirty to sixty Makassan vessels were making this voyage each year with crews of mostly Makassar and Bugis speakers numbering no fewer than 1000 men.[13] Sailing to northern Australia on the north-west monsoon in December and returning on the south-east trade wind in March and April, these crews came to fill their hulls with trepang, pearl shell, beeswax and ironwood for trade into China. In return for rights to harvest these commodities, they traded a variety of goods with their Indigenous hosts in Australia, including rice, tamarind, tobacco, alcohol, cloth, axes, knives and jewels.[14]

The impacts of these sustained annual exchanges with Indigenous groups living along the Kimberley and Arnhem Land coastlines were profound. Yolŋu languages in north-east Arnhem Land, for example, absorbed hundreds of loan words from the Makassar, Bugis and Malay languages, and Yolŋu ceremonial songs, dances and designs integrated elaborate accounts of Makassan people and technologies. Yolŋu communities retain enduring memories of Yolŋu individuals who voyaged to South-East Asia as crew on Makassan vessels, and to this day some families are known to have shared ancestry with Indonesian relatives in Sulawesi.[15]

The influence of Makassan contact is an iconic feature of ceremonies owned by the Warramiri, Dhal̲waŋu, Gumatj, Wangurri, Munyuku, Mad̲arrpa, Maŋgalili and Birrkili Gupapuyŋu clans within the Yirritja patrimoiety. Just as today's Yolŋu languages retain hundreds of loan words from the Makassar and Bugis languages – such as *rrupiya* (money), *bandirra* (flag), *buthulu* (bottle), lipalipa (canoe), *dhamburra* (drum) and *baŋ'kulu* (axe)[16] – the manikay series for the Dhal̲waŋu homeland of Gurrumuru contains songs with overtly Makassan subjects, including *yiki'* (knife), *ŋarali'* (tobacco), *manydjarrka* (cloth), *dhamburru* (drum), *djoliŋ* (flute), *dopulu* (playing cards), *ŋänitji* (arak), *barrundhu* (drunken fighting), *garrurru* (flag), *berratha* (rice) and *watjpalŋa* (rooster).[17] Flags of different colours are also prominent subjects in such manikay series and are often made for public display by these clans as important ceremonial items.

Originally made from imported Makassan cloth, they were initially used to mark beaches on the clan homelands where Makassan vessels were permitted to land. This usage demarcated a legal system of Yolŋu ports that regulated Makassan access to appropriate sites for landing, living and working (see below).

CLAN	COLOUR	PORT
Warramiri	Black	Dholtji Manunu
Dhal̲waŋu	Red	Gurrumurudjiki
Gumatj	Yellow	Gamburriŋgadjiki
Wangurri	Green	Minydharrŋura Wilirrŋura
Munyuku	White	Yarrinyyawuyŋu
Mad̲arrpa and Maŋgalili	White over blue	Baniyala Nikuniku Yilpara
Birrkili Gupapuyŋu	Blue	Yalakun Djulkayalŋgi Bäpadjambaŋ
Bäpayili (Sama whale hunters)	White over black	Motatj

TABLE 1: The Yolŋu maritime flag system.[18]

These flags remain so iconic in Yolŋu culture today that their colours often influence the costumes worn by clans in ceremonies and other formal events. They can also be emblazoned with Makassan imagery, such as an anchor and crossed swords on the red Dhal̲waŋu flag, and an anchor fastened with a cable on the yellow Gumatj flag. This system even retains a distinct flag for an even earlier group of entirely foreign Sama whale hunters, known to the Yolŋu as the Bäpayili, who are remembered sharing a sacred ancestral affinity for whales with their Yolŋu hosts. Their camp, called Motatj, was in the Wessel Islands chain.

For Yolŋu leaders, this entire continuum of foreign exchanges is traditionally perceived to be organised under the law of Allah or, rather, *Walitha'walitha*, which is a Yolŋu derivation of the Islamic oath that begins '*Lā 'ilāha 'Illā-llāh*' (There is no god but God).[19] It is also known that Muslim *a'immah* (religious leaders) had typically accompanied Makassan fleets to Australia and that Yolŋu leaders worked with them to negotiate fair trade deals and mediate any disputes that arose with visiting crews.[20]

While Yolŋu leaders generally welcomed the trade and goods brought by visiting Makassan crews, the way these exchanges are recorded in ceremonies still practised to this day simultaneously asserts Yolŋu sovereignty and autonomy from all such foreign influences. Whenever Makassan vessels broke the law by trespassing beyond flagged beaches, they are vividly remembered to have been repelled or devoured by the original ancestors themselves.

FAIR DEALING

Today, Indigenous leaders in Australia continue to draw on their 65,000 years of accumulated wisdom and the complex systems of law developed over countless generations for living on this continent. They continue to value the keeping of law as the most significant endeavour in life, along with their sacred relationships with ancestors and homelands, and they continue working to resolve the great upheaval visited upon Australia with the onset of British colonisation in 1788.

As shown by the even distribution of legal authority and ceremonial responsibilities that is so common in Indigenous societies and governance structures in Australia, tenets of balance, respect, interdependence and shared responsibility are fundamental to ensuring good governance, legal consistency and fair dealing in Indigenous legal systems. Peace, order and fair dealing, as historically mediated between Yolŋu leaders and Muslim a'immah, were also built on these fundamental principles and enabled Yolŋu trade with Makassan seafarers to endure for more than a century before the Commonwealth of Australia federated in 1901.

Despite the Crown's attempted erasure of Indigenous law and governance structures via discriminatory policies and practices, these structures nonetheless endure in Australia and continue to constantly adapt to new needs and circumstances. Moreover, despite the enduring disadvantages wrought upon Indigenous communities by the great injustices of colonisation, racism and assimilationist policies since 1788, Indigenous leaders still seek to enter a fair deal with the Australian Government.

As the Yirrkala Church Panels of 1962–63, the Yirrkala Bark Petitions of 1963, the Wuyal Petition of 1968, the Barunga Statement in 1988, the Elcho Island and Yirrkala Petitions in 1998, the East Arnhem Land Petition in 2008 and the Uluṟu Statement from the Heart in 2017 all indicate, Indigenous leaders continue to hold to their own legal principles in seeking a fair deal with the Commonwealth of Australia to remedy the cataclysmic imbalance created by British colonisation. They continue to call on the Australian Government for a treaty and a constitutional Voice to Parliament for Indigenous Australians.

8

THE GIFT OF LAW

The way of the ancestors is not in the past. It is not remote or distant. It manifests in many ways that we might glimpse, and once aware of it, we are drawn to it like moths to a flame.

Like Michael Jakamara Nelson's *Possum and Wallaby Dreaming* mosaic at Australia's Parliament House, Indigenous law and all its lessons are an intrinsic part of Australian life. Yet they are barely recognised by the Australian Government in any formal way. Even the very limited recognition of native title, as required by the *Native Title Act 1993*, can only be achieved with evidence that proves an ongoing connection to ancestors before British colonisation.

People who are most qualified to give evidence in native title cases before the courts are usually holders of law. Law is learnt by those who work hard throughout their lives to prove themselves worthy. They learn their ancestral songs and dance to them with sacred designs painted on their bodies and ceremonial objects. When these people choose to share their law with us, it is because they believe in the invaluable insights it can hold for everyone.

The way of the ancestors is not just a body of rules or a digest of what is and is not permitted. While those are necessary parts of any legal system, law is so much more. It is the great desire for harmony and balance, the proper comportment of a person in the world made by prolific ancestors long ago, the regard for all places and species as sacred, and the inner meanings of all known things. It is all this and much more.

Who else can explain all of this in any authentic way but Indigenous leaders themselves? This is why the overwhelming majority of Indigenous Australians want a Voice to Parliament enshrined in the Australian Constitution, as set out in the Uluru Statement from the Heart. This offer to all Australians would guarantee the place of Indigenous people and serve as an honourable basis for Australian nationhood.

Since British colonisation, the existence of Indigenous people has always been threatened. Historians documenting frontier violence towards Indigenous peoples have mapped the chilling numbers of massacres and victims:

> From the moment the British invaded Australia in 1788 they encountered active resistance from the Aboriginal and Torres Strait Islander owners and custodians of the lands. In

> the frontier wars which continued until the 1960s, massacres became a defining strategy to eradicate that resistance. As a result, thousands of Aboriginal men, women and children were killed.[1]

From the birth of the Australian Constitution in 1901 to the amendment in 1967 that gave Aboriginal and Torres Strait Islander people the right to be counted in the census, the existence of Indigenous Australians was utterly denied. The false doctrine of terra nullius – land not owned or governed by anyone – underpinned British legal doctrines that were only finally overturned by the High Court of Australia in 1992.

Throughout history, settler governments have explicitly aimed to exterminate Indigenous people, resulting in attempted genocide in Tasmania, sanctioned frontier violence, and forced removals of children under assimilation policies. Indigenous people were cast as fringe dwellers with no laws or culture of their own, and totally subjugated as wards of the state. Yet more than 230 years after the first British colony in Australia, Indigenous people survive, albeit in a largely disadvantaged state – more incarcerated than ever, their children still removed and their sacred sites repeatedly destroyed in pursuit of minerals and infrastructure development.

Indigenous Australians are not a race, and are certainly not an inferior people who could not survive the march of civilisation. These unsupported and outdated Western notions of race and social Darwinism need to die in Australia right now. Indigenous people are human beings with complex laws, ceremonies and social structures, and Indigenous societies are polities, not races.

In the end, Australia remains an anomaly among settler states around the world for its lack of a treaty with pre-existing Indigenous peoples. The monstrous injustice of seizure, dominion and lack of consent remains a stain on Australia and no honourable basis for Australia's nationhood can be secured without guaranteeing the place of Indigenous people within it. Any solution must be found beyond the limits of imported British laws and notions of race that dehumanise and dehistoricise Indigenous people.

In Australia there has been an almost comprehensive rejection of the idea that Indigenous peoples might have their own laws, traditions and customs within the bounds of federal and state legal systems. The exceptions are minor, such as the right to practise narrowly interpreted traditions and customs on Indigenous homelands in some demarcated areas, limited rights under local governance statutes and the narrow recognition afforded by the *Native Title Act 1993*. The Australian Law Reform Commission has proposed a constrained means of recognition by amending some statutes,[2] but its recommendations have largely been ignored. Only in a restricted way has the judiciary adopted this advice on the relevance of customary law in evidence and sentencing.

THE GIFT OF EXCHANGE

THE ULUṞU STATEMENT FROM THE HEART

We, gathered at the 2017 National Constitutional Convention, coming from all points of the southern sky, make this statement from the heart:

Our Aboriginal and Torres Strait Islander tribes were the first sovereign Nations of the Australian continent and its adjacent islands, and possessed it under our own laws and customs. This our ancestors did, according to the reckoning of our culture, from the Creation, according to the common law from 'time immemorial', and according to science more than 60,000 years ago.

This sovereignty is a *spiritual notion: the ancestral tie between the land, or 'mother nature', and the Aboriginal and Torres Strait Islander peoples who were born therefrom, remain attached thereto, and must one day return thither to be united with our ancestors. This link is the basis of the ownership of the soil, or better, of sovereignty.* It has never been ceded or extinguished, and co-exists with the sovereignty of the Crown.

How could it be otherwise? That peoples possessed a land for sixty millennia and this sacred link disappears from world history in merely the last two hundred years?

With substantive constitutional change and structural reform, we believe this ancient sovereignty can shine through as a fuller expression of Australia's nationhood.

Proportionally, we are the most incarcerated people on the planet. We are not an innately criminal people. Our children are aliened from their families at unprecedented rates. This cannot be because we have no love for them. And our youth languish in detention in obscene numbers. They should be our hope for the future.

These dimensions of our crisis tell plainly the structural nature of our problem. This is *the torment of our powerlessness*. We seek constitutional reforms to empower our people and take *a rightful place* in our own country. When we have power over our destiny our children will flourish. They will walk in two worlds and their culture will be a gift to their country.

We call for the establishment of a First Nations Voice enshrined in the Constitution.

Makarrata is the culmination of our agenda: *the coming together after a struggle*. It captures our aspirations for a fair and truthful relationship with the people of Australia and a better future for our children based on justice and self-determination.

> We seek a Makarrata Commission to supervise a process of agreement-making between governments and First Nations and truth-telling about our history.
>
> In 1967 we were counted, in 2017 we seek to be heard. We leave base camp and start our trek across this vast country. We invite you to walk with us in a movement of the Australian people for a better future.[3]

The Uluru Statement is, in essence, a proposal to all Australians for a social contract that removes the existential threat to the Indigenous peoples of Australia and alters the Australian Constitution to give them a say in their own affairs. This is what the Yolŋu term makarrata expresses in this context – the need to negotiate an end to historical conflicts and a settlement of grievances. This would reframe Australia as a nation that includes its Indigenous peoples.

The proposed Voice would be a body that resolves the problem of the status of Indigenous people as a small minority of around only 3 per cent of Australia's population by offering them a rightful say in the nation. Importantly, it would also be a remedy for the racial discrimination at the heart of the Australian Constitution. Section 25 is explicitly racist, while Section 51 (26) may be used by the Parliament of Australia to make laws that harm Indigenous Australians.[4]

Most Australians believe, however, that it is fair and reasonable to enshrine an Indigenous Voice to Parliament in the Australian

Constitution.[5] This offer of a social contract would give all Australians dignity and has been accepted by most of us, and so we await the enshrinement of the Voice.

The total imposition of foreign rule, laws and customs in Australia, and the idea that Indigenous Australians could be eliminated to enable this, is rejected by a vast majority of decent Australians as the basis for our nation. The Indigenous people of Australia have been here for 65,000 years. They developed the original laws of Australia and they are worthy of a place in the Australian Constitution.

EMBRACING LAW

You may be wondering what you can do individually to embrace the kind of law we have discussed in this book. While the discussions of Indigenous legal systems we have presented are indeed diverse and complex, the answers to this question are relatively simple.

First and foremost, respect everyone and everything in the knowledge that we are all related to everything else. Think before you act, and be reasonable in taking responsibility for your actions.

Remain mindful of the values of balance, respect, responsibility and personal betterment that Indigenous legal systems have carried over countless generations, and how alien Indigenous tenets of relationality and inclusivity are to Western notions of race and rivalry.

Do not assume things about people and circumstances based on their outward appearances. Instead, go slowly and take the time to respect and understand the nuances and complexities in all people, all things and all situations.

Be respectful, humble and patient in building relationships with others, and be reasonable, fair and cooperative in your dealings with them, even when you disagree or are in dispute, to maintain peace and stability in your life, your community and our world. Always choose the peaceful and conciliatory path over causing offence and aggression.

Respect the humanity and heritage of all people. Honour the ancestors of all. Care for our homes and environments. Understand our past and our present. Support your families and communities. Grow in wisdom. Build a shared future for all.

Honour the wisdom of your teachers, but remember that nature itself is the ultimate teacher. Pathways to betterment and wisdom hide in the most obvious of places, encoded in the natural order all around us, for anyone who takes care to find them. But also remember that the pathway to wisdom is arduous and requires us to face adversity with humility.

This is the way of ancestors, the Indigenous laws of Australia developed over the 65,000 years that humans have lived on this continent. The values and insights they offer for living a good life hold potential benefits for everyone and, as our own Indigenous teachers have shown us, have the capacity to make the world a better place for all.

Indigenous law – the way of the ancestors – is a gift to all Australians and the entire world. Instead of looking to our colonial past, Australia's origin story can be found here, in its own deep history.

ACKNOWLEDGEMENTS

Firstly, thank you to those now with the ancestors but living in our memories: Wenten Rubuntja, the women elders who founded the NPY Women's Council, Bessie Liddle, Daymbalipu Yunupiŋu, Djalaliŋba Yunupiŋu, Eunice Marika, G Yunupiŋu, Gulumbu Yunupiŋu, Raymattja Marika, Mandawuy Yunupiŋu, Joe Neparrŋa Gumbula, Rrikawuku Yunupiŋu, David Mowaljarlai, Spider Oobagooma, Peggy Patrick, Goowoomji (Paddy Bedford) and the members of Jirrawun Arts, the families of Bow River, Urwunjin (Roger Hart), Jimmy Hart, Sunlight Bassani, Paddy Bassani, Tony Flinders, George Monaghan, Gladys Tybingoompa, Gina Castelain, Mum Shirl (Shirley Coleen Perry Smith), and too many others to be named here.

And our thanks also to those who remain with us: MK Turner, Ned Jampijinpa Hargraves, Chocolate, Mona Thomas, Wiṯiyana Marika, Pam Ganambarr, Farrah Gumbula, Brian Djangirrawuy Gumbula-Garawirrtja, Renelle Gondarra, Wanta Jampijinpa Pawu, Diane Kerr, Paul Gordon, Paul Callaghan, Peter Williams, the families of Bow River, our close colleagues at the University of Melbourne, and many more. Finally, thanks again to our family and friends for all their love and support.

IMAGE CREDITS

Figure 1: [Side portrait of] Durmagum, a Nangiomeri [Ngen'giwumirri] man, c. 1935
Photograph by WEH Stanner
Image courtesy Australian Institute of Aboriginal and Torres Strait Islander Studies (AIATSIS)

Figure 2: *Pulyaranyi*, 2012
Wanta Pawu
Image courtesy the artist
© Wanta Pawu 2012

Figure 3: Warlpiri skin names, patri-semimoieties and semimoieties
Originally published in Aaron Corn & Wantarri Jampijinpa Patrick, 'Pulyaranyi: New Educational Contexts for Transferring Warlpiri Knowledge', *UNESCO Observatory Multi-Disciplinary Journal in the Arts*, 4(2), 2015
Reproduced with permission by Casey Schuurman, 2023
© Aaron Corn & Wanta Patrick 2015

Figure 4: Warlpiri ideal marriages and matrimoiety cycles
Originally published in Corn & Patrick, 2015
Reproduced with permission by Casey Schuurman, 2023
© Aaron Corn & Wanta Patrick 2015

Figure 5: The Southern Cross and Warlpiri law
Originally published in Corn & Patrick, 2015
Reproduced with permission by Casey Schuurman, 2023
© Aaron Corn & Wanta Patrick 2015

Figure 6: Tagai constellation
Casey Schuurman
© Casey Schuurman 2023

Figure 7: *Yolŋu Knowledge Constitution*, 2002
Joe Neparrŋa Gumbula
Originally published in Aaron Corn & Joe Neparrŋa Gumbula, 'Rom and the Academy Repositioned: Binary Models in Yolŋu Intellectual Traditions and Their Application to Wider Intercultural Dialogues', in Lynette Russell (ed.), *Boundary Writing: An Exploration of Race, Culture, and Gender Binaries in Contemporary Australia*, University of Hawai'i Press, Honolulu, 2006, pp. 170–9
© Joe Neparrŋa Gumbula 2002

Figure 8: *Yolŋu Knowledge Constitution*, 2002
Reproduced by Casey Schuurman with annotations by the authors
© Thames & Hudson Australia 2023

Figure 9: *Yolŋu Knowledge Constitution*, 2002
Reproduced by Casey Schuurman with annotations by the authors
© Thames & Hudson Australia 2023

Figure 10: Flying Emu constellation
Photograph © Peter Lieverdink 2019
Outline © Casey Schuurman & Aaron Corn 2023

Inside covers:

Front: *Possum and Wallaby Dreaming*, 1985
Michael Jakamara Nelson (1945–2020) Luritja/
Warlpiri peoples,
Acrylic on canvas
Parliament House Art Collection, Department of
Parliamentary Services, Canberra, ACT
Image courtesy Parliament House Art Collection

Back: *Yolŋu Knowledge Constitution*, 2002
Joe Neparrŋa Gumbula

See Figure 7

NOTES

INTRODUCTION

1 Fred Myers, *Pintupi Country, Pintupi Self: Sentiment, Place, and Politics among Western Desert Aborigines*, Smithsonian Institution Press, Washington, DC and Australian Institute of Aboriginal Studies, Canberra, 1986, p. 53.

2 Djambawa Marawili, Annette Kogolo & Christina Balcombe Davidson, 'The land sea can't talk; We have to talk for them', *Artlink*, 36(2), June 2016.

3 Michael Jakamara Nelson's family has requested that we return to using his full name.

4 University of Melbourne, quoting Marcia Langton, 'Every Australian student is entitled to know the truth' [Tweet], University of Melbourne, 29 July 2022, <twitter.com/UniMelb/status/1552868836315398144>.

1. PERSONAL PERSPECTIVES

1 See James Cook University Library, 'Eddie Koiki Mabo Timeline: 1980s', James Cook University website, n.d., <libguides.jcu.edu.au/mabo-timeline/1980s>.

2 Eddie Koiki Mabo, 'Land Rights in the Torres Strait', in Erik Olbrei (ed.), *Black Australians: The Prospects for Change*, Students Union, James Cook University of North Queensland, Townsville, 1982, pp. 143–8.

3 *Mabo et ors. v The State of Queensland* (1992) 175 CLR 1 at 61 ('Mabo No. 2 case'). Eddie Koiki Mabo (1937–92), James Rice and the Reverend Dave Passi were joint plaintiffs in the cases referred to as Mabo No. 1 (in the Supreme Court of Queensland) and Mabo No. 2 (in the High Court of Australia). The case had been before courts for ten years. They sought to have their native title in the island of Mer, or Murray Island, recognised at law. Mabo, the first plaintiff, did not live to see the handing-down of the High Court decision. The High Court found in their favour in a 6–1 majority decision.

4 Brennan J in *Mabo* (1992) 175 CLR 1 at 58.
5 Erik Olbrei (ed.), *Black Australians: The Prospects for Change*, Students Union, James Cook University of North Queensland, Townsville, 1982.
6 William Blackstone, 'Introduction: Of the Countries Subject to the Laws of England', *Commentaries on the Laws of England*, Clarendon Press, Oxford, 1765–70.
7 Brennan J in *Mabo* (1992) 175 CLR 1 at 469.
8 Brennan J in *Mabo* (1992) 175 CLR 1 at 42.
9 WEH Stanner, *The Dreaming & Other Essays*, Black Inc. Agenda, Melbourne, 2009, p. 20. Stanner described a duel he witnessed in the Daly River area. This remains the most detailed description of the duel that the Yolŋu call *makarraṯa*, which is practised in several cultural regions, including among the Warlpiri.
10 Stanner, p. 21.
11 Stanner, p. 21.
12 Stanner, p. 33.
13 Stanner, p. 30.
14 Stanner, p. 34.
15 WEH Stanner, *On Aboriginal Religion*, Sydney University Press, Sydney, 2014.
16 WEH Stanner, 'Some Aspects of Aboriginal Religion', in Robert B Crotty (ed.), *The Charles Strong Lectures*, EJ Brill, Leiden, 1987, pp. 14–15. Stanner cites his essay 'Religion, Totemism and Symbolism', which appears in Ronald M Berndt & Catherine H Berndt (eds), *Aboriginal Man in Australia: Essays in Honour or Emeritus Professor AP Elkin*, Angus & Robertson, Sydney, 1965, p. 235.
17 Donald Thomson, *Donald Thomson in Arnhem Land*, Miegunyah Press, Carlton, Vic., 2005, p. 204.
18 Marcia Langton, 'Medicine Square', in Ian Keen (ed.), *Being Black: Aboriginal Cultures in Settled Australia*, Canberra, Aboriginal Studies Press, 1988, pp. 220-5.
19 Nancy Williams, *The Yolŋu and Their Land: A System of Land Tenure and the Fight for Its Recognition*, AIATSIS, Canberra, 1986, pp. 8–9.
20 Ann Curthoys & Jessie Mitchell, '"Bring this paper to the Good Governor": Aboriginal Petitioning in Britain's Australian Colonies', in

Saliha Belmessous (ed.), *Native Claims: Indigenous Law against Empire, 1500–1920*, Oxford, Oxford Academic, 2011, p.187, <doi.org/10.1093/acprof:oso/9780199794850.003.0008>.

21 Uluru Statement from the Heart, Uluru, Northern Territory, 26 May 2017, Statement on the First Nations National Constitutional Convention.

22 S Fouad Ammoun, 'Separate Opinion of Vice-President Ammoun', *Western Sahara*, 16 October 1975, International Court of Justice, <icj-cij.org/public/files/case-related/61/061-19751016-ADV-01-04-EN.pdf>, p. 77.

23 Ammoun, pp. 85–6.

24 For a highly accessible historical account, see the ABC Radio broadcast 'In the Shadow of Terra Nullius, Part 1: Invisibility to Survival', transcript, *Rear Vision*, ABC RN website, 17 June 2018, <abc.net.au/radionational/programs/rearvision/in-the-shadow-of-terra-nullius-part-1/9861316>.

25 Marcia Langton, '"A Treaty Between Our Nations?", Inaugural Professorial Lecture, Chair of Australian Indigenous Studies, 11 July 2000, University of Melbourne, Melbourne', in Aden Ridgeway (ed.), *Treaty Talks: Talks Given at the ESORA and NAIDOC Week Forums: Treaty! Let's Get it Right!*, Eastern Suburbs Organisation For Reconciling Australia, Edgecliff, NSW, 2006. Version also published as Marcia Langton, 'Dominion and Dishonour: A Treaty Between Our Nations?', *Postcolonial Studies*, 4(1), 2001, pp. 13–26.

26 *Love v Commonwealth of Australia; Thoms v Commonwealth of Australia* [2020] HCA 3, 73, 263, 276 ('Love').

27 Shireen Morris, 'Love in the High Court: Implications for Indigenous Constitutional Recognition', *Federal Law Review*, 49(3), 2021, pp. 410–37.

28 Morris, p. 416.

29 Chris Clarkson et al., 'Human occupation of northern Australia by 65,000 years ago', *Nature*, 547(7663), 2017, pp. 306–10; Sandra Bowdler, '"Human occupation of northern Australia by 65,000 years ago" (Clarkson et al. 2017): A discussion', *Australian Archaeology*, 83(3), 2017, pp. 162–3; Anna Florin & Quan Hua, 'Aboriginal inhabitants of Madjedbebe, northern Australia used different ways to adapt

to environmental change', ANSTO website, 3 June 2022, <ansto.gov.au/news/aboriginal-inhabitants-of-madjedbebe-northern-australia-used-different-ways-to-adapt-to>.

30 Yothu Yindi, 'Treaty', on *Tribal Voice* [CD], Mushroom, Melbourne, 1991.

31 'ICTM Study Group on Indigenous Music and Dance', International Council for Traditional Music website, n.d., <ictmusic.org/group/indigenous-music-dance>.

32 Aaron Corn, *Reflections & Voices: Exploring the Music of Yothu Yindi with Mandawuy Yunupiŋu*, Sydney University Press, Sydney, 2009.

33 Yunupiŋu in Corn, *Reflections & Voices*, pp. 29–30.

34 Cecil Holmes (dir.), *Djalambu* [*sic*, *Djal̲umbu*] [film], AIATSIS, Canberra, 1964.

35 Soft Sands, 'Djiliwirri', composed by Joe Neparrŋa Gumbula & Ŋanganharralil Dhamarran̲dji, Kakadu Studios, 1997. See <youtube.com/watch?v=lA97fI7sfsU>.

36 Aaron Corn & Joe Neparrŋa Gumbula, '*Rom* and the Academy Repositioned: Binary Models in Yolŋu Intellectual Traditions and Their Application to Wider Intercultural Dialogues', in Lynette Russell (ed.), *Boundary Writing: An Exploration of Race, Culture, and Gender Binaries in Contemporary Australia*, University of Hawai'i Press, Honolulu, 2006, pp. 172, 187–92.

37 Aaron Corn & Wanta Patrick [Pawu], 'Pulyaranyi: New Educational Contexts for Transferring Warlpiri Knowledge', *UNESCO Observatory Multi-Disciplinary Journal in the Arts*, 4(2), 2015, <unescoejournal.com/wp-content/uploads/2020/03/4-2-3-CORN_V2.pdf>; Wanta Patrick [Pawu], Miles Holmes & Alan Box, *Ngurra-kurlu: A Way of Working with Warlpiri People*, Desert Knowledge CRC, Alice Springs, 2008.

38 Faculty of Science, University of Melbourne, 'New Indigenous Knowledge Institute Fellows Welcomed to Melbourne as the University Showcases Indigenous Knowledges from Around the World', University of Melbourne website, 12 August 2022, <science.unimelb.edu.au/about/news/new-indigenous-knowledge-institute-fellows>.

39 Paul Callaghan & Paul Gordon, *The Dreaming Path: Indigenous Thinking to Change Your Life*, Pantera Press, North Sydney, 2022.

40 University of Melbourne, quoting Marcia Langton, 'Every Australian student is entitled to know the truth' [Tweet], University of Melbourne, 29 July 2022, <twitter.com/UniMelb/status/1552868836315398144>.

2. FIRST LAW

1 Marcia Langton et al., *Too Much Sorry Business: The Submission of the Northern Territory Aboriginal Issues Unit of the Royal Commission into Aboriginal Deaths in Custody to Commissioner Elliott Johnston*, Aboriginal Issues Unit, Darwin, 1990.

2 Janice Reid & Dhambit Munuŋgurr, 'We Are Losing Our Brothers: Sorcery and Alcohol in an Aboriginal Community', *Medical Journal of Australia*, 2(4) supplement, 1977, pp. 1–5.

3 WEH Stanner, *The Dreaming & Other Essays*, Black Inc. Agenda, Melbourne, 2009, p. 58.

4 B Spencer & FJ Gillen, *The Arunta: A Study of a Stone Age People*, Macmillan, London, 1927, p. 592 ; FJ Gillen, 'Notes on Some Manners and Customs of the Aborigines of the McDonnell Ranges Belonging to the Arunta Tribe', in WB Spencer (ed.), *Report on the Work of the Horn Scientific Expedition to Central Australia, Part IV—Anthropology*, Dulau & Co., London, 1896, p. 185.

5 Stanner, pp. 57–8.

6 David H Turner, *Tradition and Transformation: A Study of Aborigines in the Groote Eylandt Area, Northern Australia*, AIATSIS, Canberra, 1974, pp. 26–30. Typographic errors in the original text have been corrected here for ease of reading.

7 Stanner, p. 58.

8 Roland M Berndt & Catherine H Berndt, *The Speaking Land: Myth and Story in Aboriginal Australia*, Inner Traditions International, Rochester, VT, 1994.

9 Nancy D Munn, *The Transformation of Subjects into Objects in Walbiri and Pitjantjatjara Myth*, University of Western Australia Press, Perth, 1970.

10 Nancy M Williams, *The Yolŋu and Their Land: A System of Land Tenure and the Fight for Its Recognition*, AIATSIS, Canberra, 1986.

11 WEH Stanner, 'The Yirrkala Case: Some General Principles of Aboriginal Land-Holding', unpublished manuscript, 1969, p. 4.

12 Bruce Rigsby & Athol Chase, 'The Sandbeach People and Dugong Hunters of Eastern Cape York Peninsula: Property in Land and Sea Country', in Nicolas Peterson & Bruce Rigsby (eds), *Customary Marine Tenure in Australia*, Sydney University Press, Sydney, 2014, pp. 322–3. See also Bruce Rigsby, 'Tribes, Diaspora People and the Vitality of Law and Custom: Some Comments', in Jim Fingleton & Julie Finlayson (eds), *Anthropology in the Native Title Era: Proceedings of a Workshop*, Native Titles Research Unit, AIATSIS, Canberra, 1995, pp. 25–7.

13 Howard Morphy, 'Landscape and the Reproduction of the Ancestral Past', in Eric Hirsch & Michael O'Hanlon (eds), *The Anthropology of Landscape: Perspectives on Place and Space*, Clarendon Press, Oxford, 1995, p. 184.

14 Morphy, pp. 184–5.

15 Morphy, pp. 184–5.

16 Anthony Redmond & Fiona Skyring, 'Exchange and Appropriation: The Wurnan Economy and Aboriginal Land and Labour at Karunjie Station, North-Western Australia', in Ian Keen (ed.), *Indigenous Participation in Australian Economies: Historical and Anthropological Perspectives*, ANU E Press, Canberra, 2010, <press-files.anu.edu.au/downloads/press/p122571/html/upfront.xhtml?referer=&page=0#>. See also Alan Rumsey, 'Aspects of Native Title and Social Identity in the Kimberleys and Beyond', *Australian Aboriginal Studies*, 1, 1996, pp. 2–10; Alan Rumsey, 'Kinship and Context among the Ngarinyin', *Oceania*, 51, 1981, pp. 181–92.

17 Redmond & Skyring.

18 Sonia Leonard et al., *Indigenous Climate Change Adaptation in the Kimberley Region of North-Western Australia: Learning from the Past, Adapting in the Future: Identifying Pathways to Successful Adaptation in Indigenous Communities*, National Climate Change Adaptation Research Facility, Gold Coast, 2013, p. 61; Bruce Shaw, *Countrymen: The Life Histories of Four Aboriginal Men as Told to Bruce Shaw*, AIATSIS, Canberra, 1986, p. 291.

19 R Hill, Miriuwung and Gajerrong Peoples, DG Hill & S Goodson, 'Miriuwung-Gajerrong Cultural Planning Framework: MG Guidelines for developing Management Plans for Conservation Parks and Nature Reserves under the Ord Final Agreement', WA Department of Environment and Conservation, Yawoorroong Miriuwung Gajerrong

Yirrgeb Noong Dawang Aboriginal Corporation and CSIRO, Perth, Kununurra, WA & Cairns, Qld, 2008, pp. 15–17; see also, Leonard et al., pp. 11, 62.

20 Leonard et al., p. 62.

21 Leonard et al., p. 64; Shaw, p. 291; Warmun Art Centre, *Joonba Junba Juju: Song and Dance Cycles of the Kimberley*, UTS Gallery, University of Technology, Sydney, 2014, <warmunart.com.au/culture/joonba/>.

22 Catherine Carr, 'What is a Rover Thomas painting?', PhD thesis, Faculty of Creative Arts, University of Wollongong, 2010, <ro.uow.edu.au/theses/3290>; see also <ngv.vic.gov.au/exhibition/rover-thomas/>.

23 Marcia Langton, 'Goowoomji's World', in Ewen McDonald (ed.), *MCA Collection, Volume One*, Museum of Contemporary Art, Sydney, 2012, p. 180.

24 Langton, p. 180.

25 Graham Cornall, cited in Langton, 'Goowoomji's World' pp. 180–1.

26 Pilbara and Kimberley Aboriginal Media, *Culture Day Stompem Ground 1998*, 1998, <ictv.com.au/video/item/8154>.

27 Andrish Saint Clare & Peggy Patrick (dirs), *Fire, Fire Burning Bright—Marnem, Marnem Dililib Benuwarrenji* [film], Jirrawun Indigenous Art Corporation, Kununurra, 2002. *Fire, Fire, Burning Bright* opened at the Perth Festival in February 2002 and at the Melbourne State Theatre in October 2002.

28 Melbourne Festival and the Neminuwarlin Performance Group in partnership with Jirrawun Aboriginal Arts, 'Fire Fire Burning Bright' [programme], Nuance Multimedia, Melbourne, 2002, p. 9.

29 Eulogy for Naangari [Dirrmingali, Barratjil] in the possession of the authors, 2022. Naangari is a 'subsection' or 'skin' name used here to show respect in referring to a person. 'Her bush name *Dirrmingali* refers to the 'brightness of the red rock of Kelly's Knob in the late afternoon. Her other name *Barratjil* belongs to women of *Naangari* skin and the eagle dreaming that goes with that skin. It refers to the way the Eagle dives to grab his prey with feet outstretched.' See Peggy Patrick artist bio, <reveal.net.au/artists/peggy-patrick-warmun-art-centre/>.

30 Daiwul Gidja Culture Group, *Daiwul Gidja Cross Cultural Awareness Program Course Notes*, Daiwul Gidja Culture Group, Kununurra, pp. 35–6.

31 Bruce Chatwin, *The Songlines*, Vintage Classics, London, 1998.
32 *Mabo et ors. v The State of Queensland* (1992) 175 CLR 1 at 58 ('Mabo No. 2 case').
33 Australian Government, Australian Law Reform Commission, *Connection to Country: Review of the Native Title Act 1993* (Cth), ALRC Report 126, Australian Law Reform Commission, Canberra, 2015, pp. 67–8; See also for discussion of *terra nullius*, Gerry Simpson, 'Mabo, International Law, Terra Nullius and the Stories of Settlement: An Unresolved Jurisprudence', *Melbourne University Law Review*, 19, 1993, p. 195b.

3. EVERYTHING IS RELATED

1 Aaron Corn & Wanta Patrick [Pawu], 'Pulyaranyi: New Educational Contexts for Transferring Warlpiri Knowledge', *UNESCO Observatory Multi-Disciplinary Journal in the Arts*, 4(2), 2015, p. 20.
2 Joy McCann & Anna Hough with Dianne Heriot, 'The 30th Anniversary of Australia's Parliament House: Construction of Parliament House, 1981–1987', Parliament of Australia website, n.d., <aph.gov.au/25th_Anniversary_Chronology/Construction_of_Parliament_House>.
3 Corn & Patrick, p. 8.
4 Corn & Patrick, p. 6.
5 Corn & Patrick, p. 6; Wanta Patrick [Pawu], Miles Holmes & Alan Box, *Ngurra-kurlu: A Way of Working with Warlpiri People*, Desert Knowledge CRC, Alice Springs, 2008.
6 Corn & Patrick, p. 19.
7 Cf. Laurent Dousset, 'Systems in Geography or Geography of Systems? Attempts to Represent Spatial Distributions of Australian Social Organisation', in Patrick McConvell, Piers Kelly & Sébastien Lacrampe (eds), *Skin, Kin and Clan: The Dynamics of Social Categories in Indigenous Australia*, ANU Press, Acton, ACT, 2018, pp. 43–83.
8 Cf. Aaron Corn & Joe Neparrŋa Gumbula, '*Rom* and the Academy Repositioned: Binary Models in Yolŋu Intellectual Traditions and Their Application to Wider Intercultural Dialogues', in Lynette Russell (ed.), *Boundary Writing: An Exploration of Race, Culture, and Gender Binaries in*

Contemporary Australia, University of Hawai'i Press, Honolulu, 2006, pp. 170–9.

9 RH Mathews, *Notes on the Aborigines of New South Wales*, Government Printer, Sydney, 1907, p. 116.

10 Lauriston Sharp, 'Semi-Moieties in North-Western Queensland', *Oceania*, 6(2), 1935, pp. 158–74.

11 Corn & Gumbula.

12 Mathews, p. 116.

13 Corn & Patrick, p. 9.

14 The *Janamiljarnpa* generational moiety contains the Jungarrayi, Nungarrayi, Jangala, Nangala, Jupurrula, Nupurrula, Japanangka and Napanangka skin names, while *Ngunarntarrka* contains the Jakamarra, Nakamarra, Japaljarri, Napaljarri, Jampijinpa, Nampijinpa, Japangardi and Napangardi skin names.

15 Corn & Patrick, p. 11.

16 Corn & Patrick, pp. 10–13.

17 Corn & Patrick, p. 12.

18 Nonie Sharp, *Stars of Tagai: the Torres Strait Islanders*, Aboriginal Studies Press, Canberra, 1993; Martin Nakata, 'The Cultural Interface of Islander and Scientific Knowledge', *Australian Journal of Indigenous Education*, 39(Supplement), 2010, pp. 53–7.

19 Dave Passi & Nonie Sharp, 'Meriam Sea Rights and the Resonance of Tradition: Why We Meriam People Want Sea Rights and Echoes of the Sea and the Resonance of Tradition', in Graeme K Ward & Adrian Muckle (eds), *The Power of Knowledge, The Resonance of Tradition: Electronic Publication of Papers from the AIATSIS Indigenous Studies Conference, September 2001*, AIATSIS, Canberra, 2001.

20 Duane W Hamacher et al., '"Dancing with the Stars": Astronomy and Music in the Torres Strait' in Nicholas Campion & Chris Impey (eds), *Imagining Other Worlds: Explorations in Astronomy and Culture*, Sophia Centre Press, Lampeter, UK, 2018.

21 Sharp, 1993; Peter Eseli, 'Eseli's Notebook', in Anna Shnukal & Rod Mitchell (eds), *Aboriginal and Torres Strait Islander Studies Unit Research Report Series*, 3, University of Queensland, St Lucia, 1998; Hamacher et al.

22 Jeremy Beckett, *Torres Strait Islanders: Custom and Colonialism*, Cambridge University Press, Cambridge & Sydney, 1987.
23 Duane W Hamacher with elders and knowledge holders Ghillar Michael Anderson, John Barsa, David Bosun, Ron Day, Segar Passi & Alo Tapim, *The First Astronomers: How Indigenous Elders Read the Stars*, Allen & Unwin, Crows Nest, NSW, 2022, pp. 24–5; see also Duane W Hamacher, 'A Shark in the Stars: Astronomy and Culture in the Torres Strait', *The Conversation*, 10 July, 2013, <theconversation.com/a-shark-in-the-stars-astronomy-and-culture-in-the-torres-strait-15850>.
24 DW Hamacher, 'The Moon Plays an Important Role in Indigenous Culture and Helped Win a Battle over Sea Rights', *The Conversation*, 12 February 2021.
25 Hamacher et al., p. 6.
26 Hamacher et al., p. 7.

4. RESPECT AND RESPONSIBILITY

1 Bernard Sullivan (dir.), *Yindyamarra Yambuwan (Respect Everything)* [film], Murray Art Museum Albury, 2015, <vimeo.com/140548913>.
2 Charles Sturt University, 'Our Ethos: Indigenous Commitment', Charles Sturt University website, 2022, <about.csu.edu.au/our-university/ethos>.
3 Michael Christie & Matthew Campbell, 'More than a Roof Overhead: Consultations for Better Housing Outcomes, Sub-Project 1 of the ARC Linkage Project More Than a Roof Overhead', Northern Institute, Charles Darwin University, 2013, <cdu.edu.au/centres/yaci/projects_housing.htm>, p. 10.
4 Aaron Corn & Wanta Patrick [Pawu], 'Pulyaranyi: New Educational Contexts for Transferring Warlpiri Knowledge', *UNESCO Observatory Multi-Disciplinary Journal in the Arts*, 4(2), 2015, pp. 18–20.
5 Ian Keen, *Knowledge and Secrecy in an Aboriginal Religion*, Oxford University Press, Oxford, 1994, pp. 94–5.
6 Patrick Dodson, Yawuru Registered Native Title Body Corporate, cited in Mandy Yap & Eunice Yu, *Bankwest Curtin Economics Centre Research Report*, 3(16), 2016, <bcec-community-wellbeing-from-the-ground-up-a-yawuru-example.pdf (curtin.edu.au)>, p. 28.

7 Aaron Corn & Joe Neparrŋa Gumbula, '*Rom* and the Academy Repositioned: Binary Models in Yolŋu Intellectual Traditions and Their Application to Wider Intercultural Dialogues', in Lynette Russell (ed.), *Boundary Writing: An Exploration of Race, Culture, and Gender Binaries in Contemporary Australia*, University of Hawai'i Press, Honolulu, 2006, pp. 170–9; Aaron Corn, 'Land, Song, Constitution: Exploring Expressions of Ancestral Agency, Intercultural Diplomacy and Family Legacy in the Music of Yothu Yindi with Mandawuy Yunupiŋu', *Popular Music*, 29(1), 2010, p. 85. See also Frances Morphy, 'Performing Law: The Yolŋu of Blue Mud Bay Meet the Native Title Process', in Benjamin R Smith & Frances Morphy (eds), *The Social Effects of Native Title: Recognition, Translation, Coexistence*, Research Monograph 27, ANU E Press, Canberra, 2007.

8 Franca Tamisari, 'Body, Vision and Movement: In the Footprints of the Ancestors', *Oceania*, 68(4), 1998, pp. 250–1.

9 Tamisari, pp. 249–70.

10 Tamisari, p. 251.

11 Aaron Corn & Joe Neparrŋa Gumbula, '"Now Balanda Say We Lost Our Land in 1788": Challenges to the Recognition of Yolŋu Law in Contemporary Australia', in Marcia Langton, Maureen Tehan, Lisa Palmer & Kathryn Shain (eds), *Honour Among Nations? Treaties and Agreements with Indigenous People*, Melbourne University Press, Melbourne, 2004, pp. 105–7.

12 Aaron Corn, 'Ancestral, Corporeal, Corporate: Traditional Yolŋu Understandings of the Body Explored', *Borderlands*, 7(2), 2008, p. 11.

13 Ian Keen, *Knowledge and Secrecy in an Aboriginal Religion*, Oxford University Press, Oxford, 1994, pp. 94–103.

14 Corn, 'Land, Song, Constitution', p. 85.

15 Howard Morphy, 'From Dull to Brilliant: The Aesthetics of Spiritual Power among the Yolŋu', *Man*, 24(1), 1989, pp. 21–40.

16 Corn & Patrick, p. 9.

17 Tracks Dance Company, 'Milpirri Banners', Tracks Dance Company, Darwin, <tracksdance.com.au/milpirri-banners-home-page>.

18 Aaron Corn, *Reflections & Voices: Exploring the Music of Yothu Yindi with Mandawuy Yunupiŋu*, Sydney University Press, Sydney, 2009, p. 37.

19 Mandawuy Yunupiŋu & Aaron Corn, 'Yothu Yindi: A Legacy of Hope', 28th National Conference of the Musicological Society of Australia, Sydney, 28 September 2005.
20 G Yunupiŋu considers the unfulfilled promises of subsequent prime ministers and the presentation of the East Arnhem Land Petition to Kevin Rudd in July 2008 in G Yunupiŋu 'Rom-Wat̲aŋu: The Law of the Land', *The Monthly*, July 2016, p. 29; and also in G Yunupiŋu, *Tradition, Truth and Tomorrow*, Black Inc., Collingwood, Victoria, 2015, pp. 14–21, 28–34.
21 Barbara Glowczewski, 'From Academic Heritage to Aboriginal Priorities: Anthropological Responsibilities', *Les Actes de colloques du Musée du Quai Branly Jacques Chirac*, 4, 2014, <doi.org/10.4000/actesbranly.526>, §10.
22 This has been explored in Katelyn Barney (ed.), *Collaborative Ethnomusicology: New Approaches to Music Research between Indigenous and Non-Indigenous Australians*, Lyrebird Press, Melbourne, 2014; Aaron Corn, 'Joe Gumbula, the Ancestral Chorus, and the Value of Indigenous Knowledges', *Preservation, Digital Technology & Culture*, 47(3–4), 2018, pp. 77–90; Samuel Curkpatrick, 'Soundings on a Relational Epistemology: Encountering Indigenous Knowledge through Interwoven Experience', *Journal of Intercultural Studies*, 44(5), 2023 (in press); Sally Treloyn, 'Approaching an Epistemic Community of Applied Ethnomusicology in Australia: Intercultural Research on Australian Aboriginal Song', in Klisala Harrison (ed.), *Applied Ethnomusicology in Institutional Policy and Practice*, Helsinki Collegium for Advanced Studies, Helsinki, 2016, pp. 23–39.
23 See Yunupiŋu, 'Rom-Wat̲aŋu', pp. 19–20; Yunupiŋu, *Tradition, Truth and Tomorrow*, pp. 4–8.
24 Corn & Gumbula, p. 176.
25 Corn & Gumbula, p. 184.
26 Georgia Curran, 'The "Expanding Domain" of Warlpiri Initiation Ceremonies', in Yasmine Musharbash & Marcus Barber (eds), *Ethnography and the Production of Anthropological Knowledge*, ANU E Press, Canberra, 2011, pp. 40–1.
27 Corn & Gumbula, pp. 183–5.

28 Nancy Williams, *The Yolŋu and Their Land: A System of Land Tenure and the Fight for Its Recognition*, AIATSIS, Canberra, 1986, p. 45.
29 Corn & Gumbula, p. 185.
30 Corn & Gumbula, pp. 175–83.
31 Howard Morphy, *Ancestral Connections: Art and an Aboriginal System of Knowledge*, University of Chicago Press, Chicago, 1991, pp. 66–7.
32 Williams, pp. 66–70; Keen, pp. 62–100; Michael Cooke (ed.), *Aboriginal Languages in Contemporary Contexts: Yolŋu-Matha at Galiwin'ku*, Batchelor College, Batchelor, 1996, pp. 65–85; Don Williams, *Exploring Aboriginal Kinship*, Curriculum Development Centre, Canberra, 1981.
33 Tamisari, pp. 260-1.
34 Morphy, p. 59.
35 Aboriginal Resource and Development Services, 'Native Title: The Basis of Land Ownership', Information Paper no. 5, ARDS, Darwin, 2002; Aaron Corn, 'Ancestral, Corporeal, Corporate: Traditional Yolŋu Understandings of the Body Explored', *Borderlands*, 7(2), 2008, p. 10; G Yunupiŋu, 'We Know These Things to be True: The Third Vincent Lingiari Memorial Lecture, 20 August 1998', *Journal of Australian Indigenous Issues*, 1(4), 1998, pp. 4–17.
36 Commonwealth of Australia, *Unlocking the Future: The Report of the Inquiry into the Reeves Review of the Aboriginal Land Rights (Northern Territory) Act 1976*, House of Representatives Standing Committee on Aboriginal and Torres Strait Islander Affairs, Canberra, 1999; J Reeves, *Building on Land Rights for the Next Generation: The Review of the Aboriginal Land Rights (Northern Territory) Act 1976*, 2nd edn, Aboriginal and Torres Strait Islander Commission, Canberra, 1998; RI Levitus, DF Martin & DP Pollack, 'Regionalisation of Northern Territory Land Councils', Centre for Aboriginal Economic Policy Research, Discussion Paper no. 192, Australian National University, Canberra, 1999; DF Martin, 'Report to the Hon. Robert Tickner Regarding the Proposal to Establish the North East Arnhem Ringgitj Land Council', Aboriginal and Torres Strait Islander Commission, Canberra, 1995.
37 Aboriginal Resource and Development Services, 'Native Title'; Williams, pp. 79, 88–9.

38 Samuel Curkpatrick, *Singing Bones: Ancestral Creativity and Collaboration*, Sydney University Press, Sydney, 2020, pp. 82–5.
39 Keen, p. 140.
40 Aaron Corn & Joe Neparrŋa Gumbula, 'Bu<u>d</u>utthun ratja wiyinymirri: Formal flexibility in the Yolŋu manikay tradition and the challenge of recording a complete repertoire' *Australian Aboriginal Studies*, 2, 2007, p. 123.

5. FAMILY BUSINESS

1 Mischa B Adams, 'Who is David Gulpilil?', <gulpilil.com/biography.htm>, 2001; Ryan Gilbey, 'David Gulpilil Obituary', *The Guardian*, 14 December 2021, <theguardian.com/film/2021/dec/13/david-gulpilil-obituary>; Garry Maddox, 'David Dalaithngu [Dalaythŋu] Was a Mesmerising Movie Presence', *The Sydney Morning Herald*, 29 November 2021, <smh.com.au/culture/movies/david-gulpilil-was-a-mesmerising-movie-presence-20210325-p57dwd.html>.
2 Rolf de Heer, Peter Djigirr & the people of Ramingining (dirs), *Ten Canoes*, Film Finance Corporation Australia and Fandango Australia/Vertigo Productions, in association with the South Australian Film Corporation, the Adelaide Film Festival & SBS Independent, Sydney, Australia, 2006. Peter Djigirr is an actor, director and producer. He co-directed *Ten Canoes* and was a producer for *Charlie's Country*, directed by Rolf de Heer (2013). He is also a Gurruwiling [Gurruwiliŋ] Ranger for the Southeast Arafura Catchment. See also, *Ten Canoes: Interview with Peter Djigirr*, Vertigo, London, 2007.
3 Nicolas Roeg (dir.), *Walkabout* [film], Max L Raab-Si Litvinoff Films, 1971.
4 Henri Safran & Ian Goddard (dirs), *Storm Boy*, South Australia Film Corporation, Adelaide, 1976.
5 For further reading on the making of *Ten Canoes*, see Margot Duband and Clémentine Débrosse, '*Ten Canoes*: A Film Between Historical Reenactment, Myths and Fiction', *CASOAR Arts et Anthropologie de l'Océanie*, 15 April 2021, <casoar.org/en/2021/04/15/ten-canoes-entre-reconstitution-historique-mythes-et-fiction/>; Libby Tudball & Robert Lewis, *Ten Canoes: ATOM Study Guide*, Australian Teachers of Media,

2006, <theeducationshop.com.au/downloads/atom-study-guides/ten-canoes-atom-study-guide/>.

6 Palace Films, 'Ten Canoes Press Kit', Palace Films, Balwyn, Vic., 2006, p. 4.

7 DF Thomson, 'Notes on Some Primitive Watercraft in Northern Australia', *Man*, 52, 1952, pp. 1–5; DF Thomson, 'Two Devices for the Avoidance of First-Cousin Marriage among the Australian Aborigines', *Man*, 55, 1955, pp. 39–40.

8 Ian Keen, 'The Evolution of Australian Kin Terminologies: Models, Conditions, and Consequences', *Current Anthropology*, 63(1), 2022, pp. 31–67; John F Martin & P Govinda Reddy, 'Gidjingali and Yolŋu Polygyny: Age Structure and the Control of Marriage', *Oceania*, 57(4), 1987, pp. 243–60; Benjamin R Smith, 'Sorcery and the Dividual in Australia', *Journal of the Royal Anthropological Institute*, 22(3), 2016, pp. 670–87.

9 WEH Stanner, 'The Boyer Lectures: After the Dreaming', in *The Dreaming & Other Essays*, Black Inc. Agenda, Melbourne, 2009, pp. 172–224.

10 Festival de Cannes, 'Glossary and Explanations' in *Ten Canoes: A Film by Rolf de Heer*, Festival de Cannes, Official Selection (booklet), <cdn-media.festival-cannes.com/film_film/0002/36/3c0f86d423053c31a532a39a88b6c6c9c4db2ddb.pdf>.

11 Palace Films, p. 4.

12 Christine Judith Nicholls, 'Songlines: Tracking the Seven Sisters Is a Must-Visit Exhibition for All Australians', *The Conversation*, 20 December 2017.

13 Molly Reynolds, Tania Nehme & Rolf de Heer (dirs), *The Balanda and the Bark Canoes: The Making of Ten Canoes* [film], Film Australia, Lindfield, NSW, 2006.

14 W Lloyd Warner, *A Black Civilization: A Social Study of an Australian Tribe*, Harper & Brothers, New York, 1958, p. 144 passim.

15 Palace Films, p. 4.

16 Palace Films, p. 5.

17 Palace Films, p. 5.

6. GENDERED BUSINESS

1 Robert Tonkinson, 'Semen versus Spirit-Child in a Western Desert Culture', in LR Hiatt (ed.), *Australian Aboriginal Concepts*, AIATSIS, Canberra & Humanities Press, Atlantic Highlands, NJ, 1978; Emma Lawson & Rosemary Bolger, '"Don't be afraid": Tiwi Sistergirls Spread Acceptance through Traditional Dance', SBS News, 23 November 2019.

2 The resources are available on the 'Shop' page of the NPY Women's Council website: <npywc.org.au/shop/>; See also Ngaanyatjarra Pitjantjatjara Yankunytjatjara Women's Council Aboriginal Corporation, *Traditional Healers of Central Australia*, Magabala Books, Broome, WA, 2013.

3 Phyllis Kaberry, *Aboriginal Woman: Sacred and Profane*, Routledge, Abingdon-on-Thames, UK, 2003.

4 Diane Bell, *Daughters of the Dreaming*, 2nd edn, Allen & Unwin, St Leonards, NSW, 1993.

5 Bangarra Dance Theatre Australia, 'Terrain: Study Guide', Bangarra Dance Theatre Australia, Sydney, 2016, <bangarra.com.au/media/rhwnuutu/final_terrain_studyguide_2012-002.pdf>, p. 11.

6 Frances Rings, 'Choreographer's Notes: Terrain', *Bangarra Dance Theatre Knowledge Ground*, Bangarra Dance Theatre, <bangarra-knowledgeground.com.au/productions/terrain/choreographers-notes>; Frances Rings & Shane Carroll, 'Interview with Frances Rings: Terrain', produced by Tiffany Parker, Bangarra Dance Theatre, 2015, <bangarra-knowledgeground.com.au/productions/terrain/interview-with-frances-rings-terrain>.

7 Rachel Perkins, 'Songs to Live By', *The Monthly*, 1 July 2016.

8 Perkins, 2016.

9 Perkins, 2016.

10 Myfany Turpin, 'Finding Arrernte Songs', in Jim Wafer & Myfany Turpin (eds), *Recirculating Songs: Revitalising the Singing Practices of Indigenous Australia*, Asia-Pacific Linguistics, School of Culture, History and Language, College of Asia and the Pacific, Australian National University, Canberra, 2017, pp. 90–102.

11 Perkins, citing Myfany Turpin, 'Arrente Women's Songs Today', About Music Lecture, Sydney Conservatorium of Music, University of Sydney, 27 July 2015.
12 Perkins, 2016.
13 Perkins, 2016.
14 Perkins, 2016.
15 Perkins, 2016. As TGH Strehlow's work (*Songs of Central Australia*, Angus & Robertson, Sydney, 1971) is restricted to initiated Aboriginal men. Perkins read the contents page and found a few pages at the end of the book referring to women's songs; she cites Strehlow's words from this section of the book.
16 Perkins, 2016.
17 Perkins, 2016.
18 Marcia Langton, Nina Fitzgerald & Amba-Rose Atkinson et al., *Welcome to Country: A Travel Guide to Indigenous Australia*, 2nd edn, Hardie Grant Travel, Richmond, Victoria, 2021, pp. 120–1.
19 Langton et al., pp. 120–1.
20 Deborah Bird Rose, *Nourishing Terrains: Australian Aboriginal Views of Landscape and Wilderness*, Australian Heritage Commission, Canberra, 1996.
21 Marcia Langton, 'The Hindmarsh Island Bridge Affair: How Aboriginal Women's Religion Became an Administerable Affair', *Australian Feminist Studies*, 11(24), 1996, pp. 211–17.
22 Marcia Langton, 'Homeland: Sacred Visions and the Settler State', *Artlink*, 20(1), 2000, pp. 11–16.
23 See John Leslie Toohey & Department of Aboriginal Affairs, *Seven Years On: Report by Mr Justice Toohey to the Minister for Aboriginal Affairs on the Aboriginal Land Rights (Northern Territory) Act 1976 and Related Matters*, Australian Government Publishing Service, Canberra, 1984.
24 Marcia Langton, 'Grandmothers' Law, Company Business and Succession in Changing Aboriginal Land Tenure Systems', in G Yunupingu (ed.), *Our Land is Our Life: Land Rights Past, Present and Future*, University of Queensland Press, St Lucia, Queensland, 1997, pp. 84–116.

25 John Woodward, *Aboriginal Land Rights Commission: Second Report*, Commonwealth of Australia, Canberra, ACT, 1974.
26 Catherine H Berndt, *Women's Changing Ceremonies in Northern Australia*, Hermann, Paris, 1950.
27 Nicholas Peterson, 'Rights, Residence and Process in Australian Territorial Organisation' in Nicolas Peterson & Marcia Langton (eds), *Aborigines, Land and Land Rights*, AIATSIS, Canberra, 1983, pp. 140–3.

7. WISDOM AND LEADERSHIP

1 Aaron Corn & Wanta Patrick [Pawu], 'Pulyaranyi: New Educational Contexts for Transferring Warlpiri Knowledge', *UNESCO Observatory Multi-Disciplinary Journal in the Arts*, 4(2), 2015, p. 2.
2 Corn & Patrick, p. 11.
3 Aaron Corn, 'Joe Gumbula, the Ancestral Chorus, and the Value of Indigenous Knowledges', *Preservation, Digital Technology & Culture*, 47(3–4), 2018, pp. 79–89.
4 Franca Tamisari, 'Body, Vision and Movement: In the Footprints of the Ancestors', *Oceania*, 68(4), 1998, p. 251.
5 Ngaanyatjarra Pitjantjatjara Yankunytjatjara Women's Council Aboriginal Corporation, *Traditional Healers of Central Australia*, Magabala Books, Broome, WA, 2013.
6 Zena Cumpston, Michael-Shawn Fletcher & Lesley Head, *Plants: Past, Present and Future*, Thames & Hudson Australia, Port Melbourne, 2022.
7 Faculty of Science, University of Melbourne, 'New Indigenous Knowledge Institute Fellows Welcomed to Melbourne as the University Showcases Indigenous Knowledges from Around the World', University of Melbourne website, 12 August 2022, <science.unimelb.edu.au/about/news/new-indigenous-knowledge-institute-fellows>.
8 Corn & Patrick, p. 13.
9 Wanta Patrick [Pawu], in Stewart Carter & Wanta Jampijinpa Patrick [Pawu] (dirs), *Milpirri: Winds of Change* [film], PAW Media & People Pictures, Yuendumu, 2012.
10 Corn & Patrick, pp. 6–7.

11 Terry Yumbulul & Keith Djiniyini, 'My Island Home: A Marine Protection Strategy for Manbuynga ga Rulyapa (Arafura Sea)', in G Yunupiŋu (ed.), *Our Land is Our Life: Land Rights Past, Present and Future*, University of Queensland Press, St Lucia, Queensland, 1997, pp. 181–7; see also Frances Morphy et al., 'Toponyms from 3000 Years Ago? Implications for the History and Structure of the Yolŋu Social Formation in North-east Arnhem Land', *Archaeology in Oceania*, 55(3), 2020, pp. 153–67.

12 Anne Clarke & Ursula Frederick, 'Making a Sea Change', in Martin Thomas & Margo Neale (eds), *Exploring the Legacy of the 1948 Arnhem Land Expedition*, ANU E Press, Canberra, 2011, p. 151; Aaron Corn & Brian Djangirrawuy Garawirrtja, 'The Legacy of Yolŋu Makassan Contact: Before the First Wave', in Gillian Dooley & Danielle Clode (eds), *The First Wave: Exploring Early Coastal Contact History in Australia*, Wakefield Press, Adelaide, 2019, p. 110.

13 Campbell Macknight, 'Studying Trepangers', in Marshall Clark & Sally K May (eds), *Macassan History and Heritage: Journeys, Encounters and Influences*, ANU Press, Canberra, 2013, p. 30.

14 GW Earl, 'On the Aboriginal Tribes of the Northern Coast of Australia', *Journal of the Royal Geographical Society of London*, 16, 1846; Campbell Macknight, *The Voyage to Marege'*, Melbourne University Press, Carlton, Vic., 1976.

15 Michael Cooke, 'The Macassan Influence', in Michael Cooke (ed.), *Aboriginal Languages in Contemporary Contexts: Yolngu Matha at Galiwin'ku*, Batchelor College, Batchelor, NT, 1996, pp. 1–20.

16 Cooke.

17 Peter G Toner, 'When the Echoes Are Gone: A Yolŋu Musical Anthropology', PhD dissertation, Australian National University, 2001, pp. 79–80, 259–72.

18 Aaron Corn, 'Before the First Wave: Understanding the Intersection of Yolŋu Expressions of Makassan Contact Histories and Independence from Foreign Influences in Northeast Arnhem Land', in G Dooley & D Clode (eds), *The First Wave: Exploring Early Coastal Contact History in Australia*, Wakefield, Adelaide, 2019, pp. 106–34.

19 Ian S McIntosh, 'The Ship's Mast', *The Beagle*, 15, 1999, p. 156.

20 This was first deduced by Ronald M Berndt & Catherine H Berndt in *Arnhem Land: Its History and Its People*, Cheshire, Melbourne, 1954, p. 46.

8. THE GIFT OF LAW

1 Lyndall Ryan et al., *Colonial Frontier Massacres in Australia, 1788–1930*, Centre for 21st Century Humanities, University of Newcastle website, n.d., <c21ch.newcastle.edu.au/colonialmassacres/>.

2 Australian Government, Australian Law Reform Commission, *Recognition of Aboriginal Customary Laws*, ALRC Report 31, Australian Law Reform Commission, Canberra, 1986. See also Northern Territory Law Reform Commission, 'Report of the Committee of Inquiry into Aboriginal Customary Law: Report on Aboriginal Customary Law', *Australian Indigenous Law Reporter*, 8(3), 2003, pp. 91–6; Northern Territory Law Reform Committee, Report 46, *Two Justice Systems Working Together: Report on the Recognition of Local Aboriginal Laws in Sentencing and Bail*, Report 46, November 2020, <justice.nt.gov.au/__data/assets/pdf_file/0011/977546/report-recognition-local-aboriginal-laws-sentencing-bail.pdf>; Law Reform Commission of Western Australia, *Aboriginal Customary Laws: The Interaction of Western Australian Law with Aboriginal Law and Culture: Final Report*, Law Reform Commission of Western Australia, Perth, 2006, <indigenousjustice.gov.au/resources/aboriginal-customary-laws-final-report-the-interaction-of-western-australian-law-with-aboriginal-law-and-culture/>.

3 'About the Voice: What Is the Uluṟu Statement?', From the Heart website, 2022, <fromtheheart.com.au/%20explore-the-uluru-statement/>. Further information at Commonwealth of Australia, National Indigenous Australians Agency, *Indigenous Voice Co-design Process Final Report to the Australian Government*, Commonwealth of Australia, Canberra, 2021, <voice.niaa.gov.au/final-report>.

4 Australian Government, Department of Families, Housing, Community Services and Indigenous Affairs, *Constitutional Recognition of Indigenous Australians*, Department of Families, Housing, Community Services and

Indigenous Affairs, Canberra, 2011. See also Robert French, 'The Race Power: A Constitutional Chimera', in Hoong P Lee & George Winterton (eds), *Australian Constitutional Landmarks*, Cambridge University Press, Cambridge, UK, 2003, pp. 180–212; *Kartinyeri v Commonwealth* (1998), HCA 22, 195 CLR 337 at 81–5, per Gummow and Hayne JJ; Dylan Lino, 'Replacing The Race Power: A Reply to Pritchard', *Australian Indigenous Law Review*, 15(2) 2011, pp. 58–63; Sarah Pritchard, 'The "Race" Power in Section 51(Xxvi) of The Constitution', *Australian Indigenous Law Review*, 15(2), 2011, pp. 44–57.

5 The Australia Institute conducted a poll in June and July 2022, reporting that 'nearly two in three Australians (65%) surveyed in July would vote "Yes" to enshrine a Voice to Parliament for First Nations peoples in the Constitution'. The Australia Institute, 'Polling – Voice to Parliament in the Constitution', 31 July 2022, <australiainstitute.org.au/report/polling-voice-to-parliament-in-the-constitution/>.

INDEX

Note: Page numbers in **bold** refer to captions or images.

The best of both worlds

TITLES IN THE FIRST KNOWLEDGES SERIES

SONGLINES
Margo Ngawa Neale & Lynne Kelly
(2020)

DESIGN
Alison Page & Paul Memmott
(2021)

COUNTRY
Bill Gammage & Bruce Pascoe
(2021)

ASTRONOMY
Karlie Noon & Krystal De Napoli
(2022)

PLANTS
Zena Cumpston, Michael-Shawn Fletcher & Lesley Head
(2022)

LAW
Marcia Langton & Aaron Corn
(2023)

INNOVATION
Ian J McNiven & Lynette Russell
(2023)

HEALTH
Shawana Andrews, Sandra Eades & Fiona Stanley
(2024)

CEREMONY
Georgia Curran & Wesley Enoch
(2025)

POLITICS
Mary Graham & Morgan Brigg
(2026)

Published in conjunction with the National Museum of Australia
and supported by the Australia Council for the Arts.